Flame ignites the page,
A life indelibly changed:
A hope and prayer.

Eric Tinsay Valles
Author of *After the Fall: Dirges Among Ruins*

At the same time learned and passionate, Desmond Kon is the consummate Catholic poet whose "litany of sounds" will mesmerize any reader sensitive to the spiritual life or, indeed, just poetry itself. In his collection *Heart Fiat*, the poet has the self-confidence and the talent to surrender himself to the poem "as each line must carve itself into form"—indeed, as if the poem by its own intuition, even wisdom, had the power to find its way into sacredness. And as a result, we, the readers, experience something extraordinary as we feel the charged and indelible pressure of each word "like ink on skin, this heavy black." In this process of intense spiritual and physical revelation, poem and prayer become gloriously indistinguishable.

Orlando Ricardo Menes
Author of *The Gospel of Wildflowers and Weeds*

For many years I've avoided poetry, probably because I was compelled to recite it throughout high school by many white-haired professors. But now, as my own white hairs begin to show, my thirst for poetic verse has grown, mainly through reading or listening to the likes of Desmond Francis Xavier Kon Zhicheng-Mingdé and some of his contemporaries. For me, Kon's *Heart Fiat* struck some of the right chords, lifting my soul a little higher, even though the journey was somewhat shrouded in mystery. I had a full-blown chiaroscuro experience as I made way through the scenes. There were moments of immense darkness, where I was grappling to understand, or to feel a particular emotion, while other times, the light pierced through, reflecting from my mind, into my heart, turning it, a little more, from stone to flesh. This led to momentary bursts of joy or some minutes of hot therapeutic tears, and for this I'm forever grateful to Desmond. This commendation was completed on the Feast of Our Lady of Mt Carmel.

Sebastian James
Journalist of The Associated Press

In the opening poem of *Heart Fiat*, Desmond Kon explains, "I was taught the virtue of exacting strain / from the particular, / an exactitude of language… Till meaning broke." What follows are rituals of defining and trying to define, of variation within repetition, as well as ancient and contemporary narratives knotted together as epistle, list, contrition, and lament. In lyrical, experimental, and prose poems, Kon keeps unfolding meaning into a call-and-response with philosophers, theologians, poets, and saints. In these fast-moving poems—where brackets underscore thought within thought—Kon presents "no illusion / but a mirror / of what faith can become."

Marjorie Maddox
Author of *Begin with a Question*

The poems in *Heart Fiat* by Desmond Francis Xavier Kon Zhicheng-Mingdé defy easy categorization, but they can surely be called extravagant, in the true meaning of the word, "wandering outside boundaries." From their disparate forms, their wide-ranging intellectual, artistic and literary references, and the precise and surprising language, these poems demand to be reread, all the better out loud. But what truly captivated me was Kon's voice, the intimacy he offers, and the unfolding self-revelations, which are not for his sake alone, but for anyone on a companionate journey.

Maryanne Hannan
Author of *Rocking Like It's All Intermezzo: 21st Century Psalm Responsorials*

Desmond Francis Xavier Kon Zhicheng-Mingdé's collection, *Heart Fiat*, is unlike any book I have read. This striking work of confessional poetry of varied forms and subjects reflects the author's great love of language from the simple to the erudite. His rock-solid Catholic faith and devotion, very much informed by the Ignatian spirituality of his namesake, is clearly evident here. The combination of his intellectual theology with his humble and unaffected piety is so felicitous and so very refreshing in our often jaded world today. Please God, the deep ruminations and reflections in Desmond's striking collection of poetry will inspire the readers of this powerful work to ponder their own faith as seriously and as fruitfully as the author has his.

Fr Gerard Garrigan, OSB
Author of *The Sacred, The Profane, The Hodiamont*

Lifting us far beyond this earthbound life, Desmond Kon's *Heart Fiat* displays his signature grace and erudition at its best, revealing a soul shot through with the light of eternity where God resides. This collection is Kon's literary treasure trove of love offerings—poems of "bright light" guiding us through "the way of language," a realm of a faith-infused imagination where the sacraments of daily life yield wonder and awe in the presence of the Holy Spirit. The truth shimmers on these pages with an "eternal echo" in praise of Christ, the giver of all good gifts, and ultimately, our salvation.

Karen An-hwei Lee
Author of *The Beautiful Immunity* and *Phyla of Joy*

"Holy... is this moment of needing definitions," thus Desmond Kon situates his exploration of meaning in a rich Catholic topography inhabited by blessed ones and saints, pilgrims and penitent sinners. In a fascinating, all-encompassing tour where "the transcendental signified is situated, proper" there is no area beyond experience that is not imbued with the sacred, the miraculous. What a blessing it is to encounter a poet so immersed in God's Word that he may prayerfully, convincingly aver, "all things now made for this, to house our love."

Sofia M. Starnes
Virginia Poet Laureate, Emerita
Author of *The Consequence of Moonlight* and other works

As epigraph to *Geography III*, Elizabeth Bishop offers a list of questions that frame the poems to follow. Similarly, Desmond Kon frames the greater body of *Heart Fiat* with questions given in the "daily examen," a technique of prayerful reflection meant to poise the contemplative soul toward God. Rather than a geographical journey, what follows in Kon's book is something closer to a theater of the soul, one richly and responsively populated with the words and images of saints and poets, artists and theologians, scriptures and iphones, and all refracted through this exuberant poet's vibrant communion of art and prayer, his "holy song." At once sweeping and probing, venturesome and precise, the poems of *Heart Fiat* know that while there will be times "nothing seems adequate as a salve or balm," there is always before us "the great yes," as well as the joyful and bracing knowledge that "love demands an idiom."

Daniel Tobin
Author of *The Mansions*

In *Heart Fiat* Desmond Kon roams the interior and exterior world as one. The spiritual and religious are here, but these realms are passages to the mysteries of our tangible existence: the "real presence" becomes the conviction, "now I begin"; the wedding at Cana prompts Kon to ask, who is "worth my lifetime of longing." Elsewhere an account of the challenging marriage of a folk artist evokes a meditation on Saint Gertrude, who "is safe in the monastery of her own formation." If you've thought the spiritual can be safely locked away, these poems will make you think again.

Fr Tom Holahan, CSP
Creative Consultant of Paulist Productions

This is the city of the mind after the Fall. After tyrannous empires die and come to life over and over to torment us. After the Bomb, its constant curse threatening our fragile peace. In these days of diaspora when the sons and daughters of men and women scrabble for survival on the edges of inhospitable borderlands. In these times when language is a mere bundle of flippant clichés without meaning. How does one create poetry in this bleak landscape? With the heart's fiat, with faith, finding God's tracks among the rubble of words, shards of history, splinters of memory. He is there, still there, heart fiat says.

Merlie M. Alunan
Professor Emeritus
Author of *Tigom: Collected Poems*

Many poems in *Heart Fiat* are stunning, and together they create an illumination, utterly inspired by God. This collection's beauty lies in its inherent purposes—to celebrate living and wonder about the relationship between poetry and the divine: "Petitions. Or, to ask: When does prayer become a poem, and a poem a prayer?" As these poems inquire and consider answers, readers encounter other voices—everyone from the Saints to Monet to the Serbian American poet Charles Simic. *Heart Fiat* employs multiple forms, some hybrid, and all with a contemporary bent. The combination leaves the reader awed at Kon's facility to use form and language for the highest expression, forming a riot of Love.

Kimberly K. Williams
Author of *Still Lives* and *Sometimes a Woman*

HEART FIAT

POEMS

DESMOND FRANCIS XAVIER
KON ZHICHENG-MINGDÉ

HEART FIAT
Poems

Resource Publications
An Imprint of Wipf and Stock Publishers
199 W. 8th Ave., Suite 3
Eugene, OR 97401

www.wipfandstock.com

PAPERBACK ISBN: 979-8-3852-2982-6
HARDCOVER ISBN: 979-8-3852-2983-3
EBOOK ISBN: 979-8-3852-2984-0

Book design by J. R. Padua.

F. X.

AMA ET QUOD VIS FAC

CONTENTS

Be who God meant you to be,
and you will set the world on fire.

Saint Catherine of Siena

DAILY
EXAMEN

RETROSPECT

Catachresis, Then Catechesis

"Friends, do not be afraid of silence or stillness."

Pope Benedict XVI

How much can you stretch that note,
across the page,
line scored with blood from finger and lip
—bloodied, hoarse throat?

I was taught the virtue of exacting strain
from the particular,
an exactitude of language habitude/attitude.

I was taught stress was a good thing,
pressure application to hear the snap, the shattering glass.

Till meaning broke—
watch for the particular instance
of breakage.

When sense seems rent.

And, all one hears is hole,
the wholeness of the empty,
more bereft
than bereft.

How much to displace when replacing?

What of meaning, diced, spliced—no *then* utilized here,
to connote some sequence or consequence, even relevance?

I was taught so many things.

But for silence, there's the discourse of it.

But for the discourse of silence

>—there's none of it—
>—who was it who said that, as if to rejoin or echo?—
>—not even the irony—
>— who is it now, who speaks within this utterance?—

>>there is always that of holy silence.

"Friends, do not be afraid of silence or stillness."

Pope Benedict XVI said this.

There are more lines to the line.

There are more lines
>—to line the line.

>>"Listen to God."

>>[... ... ...]
>>[... ... ...]

>>"Adore Him in the Eucharist."

The Difference of Sounds

"A beautiful homily, a genuine sermon must begin with the first
proclamation, with the proclamation of salvation. There is nothing more
solid, deep and sure than this proclamation. Then you have to do catechesis."

Pope Francis

What did I think to myself
that last morning,
that last morning I remember
      as if a faraway wedge
      of wharfage?

      Sound feels like that today.

      Sounds feel,
      like that day—do they really,
      or did that just sound right?

          To position a line,
      placement
      and placemat on page.

      Sound.

      Its interiority
      a kind of evanescence,
      according to another book
      already open to an opportune page.

      Sound—
      what manner of conversation
      is its conversation
          with eternal time?

The homily has started its litany of sounds.

This morning, as with each morning, respite of consolations.

Poem Prolog:
Hereinafter, Along the Line

Every poem henceforth must be bright light,
an inner shine
like what you just heard—
                    this reflective sound.

This and that, the way of refracting something.

What is this moment to become,
an early morning ethos suddenly awake?

To its own shimmer of truth,
                        like glint
                    off a glazed plate.

To echo an echo.

To make of an article an article.

Each line within
each poem must carve itself into form.

Again, a suddenness.

Again, a repetition of what it means—
                            to be.

To iterate into being the form of truth,
how quietly formal it now all seems.

As if it was there all along,
but how I never let in the light,
                    like morning's window.

THE DAILY EXAMEN

Set aside 10 minutes for your Daily Examen.
Pause for contemplation.
Begin. Take three breaths—slow and deep breaths.
Be aware that you are in the presence of the Holy.

1. Gratitude: *What may I give praise and thanksgiving for?*
2. Petition: *What does the light of God reveal to me?*
3. Reflection: *What does my detailed review of today surface?*
4. Contrition: *What are my responses to God, given my insight?*
5. Resolution: *What may I look forward to gaining tomorrow?*

DAILY
EXAMEN

ACT I
SCENES I-XVI

The Year Ash Wednesday
Fell on Saint Valentine's Day

Lord, you know everything; you know that I love you.

This is at the end of the two-page document they gave me years ago.
It's placed after the Act of Contrition. It can be used too, said too.
It seems more comforting, but less interrogative of all my misgivings,
all that needs washing away.

I told the priest my godfather suggested weekly confession.
That's been his lifelong practice—I say practice; you say discipline,
some say habit. [Lifelong since he made the decision to join The Work.]
I told the priest that confession is palpably healing for me,
and Mass after becomes so much lighter, brighter.

+

"Lord, you know everything; you know that I love you."

When I say this, I like the feeling—
        of first deciding to say it,
        then the feeling of saying it,
            having said it,
        and the feeling that comes after.

+

Saint Peter was sad that Jesus had to ask the question three times.

Simon, son of John, do you love me?

Saint Peter must have remembered the threefold denial.
Just as the crow reminded him. Did he willingly make those denials,
with full awareness of his decision? Even with Jesus letting him know,
the prophecy already revealed? Does one recognize a prophecy as it
unpeels its moment, or does the realization only happen after the fact?

As plainly said as a matter of fact.

An afterthought,
like I keep saying these days.

+

[[[[[[How culpable is our culpability?]]]]]]

+

"Please remember—"

"Bring us the palms you've kept all year—"

"This is what Ash Wednesday looks like—"

"This is what Saint Valentine's Day looks like this year—"

"No meat, no dispensation from fasting—"

"I'll imagine Saint Valentine's relics in Dublin and Rome—"

+

[The priest at The Work said we crucify Christ still, to this day.]
[That's why we cry "Crucify, Crucify, Crucify" in the Passion Play.]

I avoid saying it,
even for the iterative drama, the enactment.

Some say it once,
then stop,
as if in sudden realization
of what it means.

+

"This is what Ash Wednesday looks like on Saint Valentine's—"

"People walking around with ash on their foreheads—"

"Ours so well-drawn, pressed deep into skin, as if inscribed—"

"It's like ink on skin, this heavy black—"

"Black as coal, these ashes from last year's Palm Sunday Mass—"

"Imagine the shape of the cross on so many foreheads—"

"Imagine the shape of the cross, all across town—"

+

[The priest at The Work said we crucify Christ, because we sin still.]

I say it now, muttered under my breath, to acknowledge our culpability.

> How guilt-smeared
> our collective culpability.

I told the priest how hard it was to live by the eight Beatitudes each day.
Every confession, there are some of the same sins, like a stubborn stain.
This, not the kind of iteration—of aesthetic—I used to like. It is not
the sort of story rhythm I'd like to remember. I remember to confess
the sins I can't remember, that these have to be washed away too.

It seems nowadays, I wait for the pews to empty. I sit for about an
hour more. I take out the prayer leaflet, *A Quarter Hour Before the
Blessed Sacrament*, and contemplate each item in the five small pages.
Sometimes, I start with the rosary first, which also takes a quarter hour.
Then, I rise and walk to the tabernacle. I kneel on the marble, and
bring my forehead to the floor.

> Three times,
> and every time,
> the same love profession.

> That's what love looks like,
> talking to Jesus
> in the tabernacle.

Lord, you know everything; you know that I love you.

Then the keys, then the rock,
        given to the loving disciple,
        the one who loved him most.

    Then,
    Jesus said to Saint Peter:

        "Feed my sheep."

Tintinnabulation

"There is no competition of sounds between a nightingale and a violin."

Dejan Stojanovic

I say *have a blessed Sunday*;
the hope is a recitation of confidence, as with liturgical chant.

Hwang In Kwon's oboe is like a reed,
the angel Gabriel standing alone, in an orchestral wind.

Every other instrument and sound wraps around the flutish.

And the responsorial emanates water, also blessed into holiness.

Everything is holy, some poet once wrote.

Holy, too, is this moment of needing definitions.

Holy, too, is looking up a word, like tintinnabulation.

Holy, too, is this practice of iteration, its own litany and rhythm.

Our eternal searching for definition,
            as with so many other human acts,
            each one a paraphrase or restatement
                        of something, beyond itself.

Tintinnabulation is a bit of onomatopoeia,
                        like the killdeer or poorwill.
Both birds whose common names reflect their call
                        —and elicit,
                                    in a way
                        the memory of a memory—
                        how I remember
the loud clang of church bells,
an invisible, anonymous celebrant behind it all.

Dear Impressionism

How the light of the world has changed—these sudden wintry weeks within the tropics. Then, the burning airlessness, turn of sweltering weather. These lily pads rest low in the basin, half the pondwater. Our boxed-in homes house herb gardens now, small straw-grasping acts, feeble attempts but hopeful nonetheless. It's the same in our churchyard, its Bible Garden with small plots of dill, coriander, mint, sage, all for the refectory table. For color, there are lilies and tulips, even wild roses.

I'm seated on a Jacobean bench. Beside me are four books:

> *Flight Behavior*
> *Odds Against Tomorrow*
> *The Overstory*
> *Get A Life*

The four titles line up to form a neat quatrain, and really, an exhortation. This is what ecofiction can do, reimagine the already seemingly unimaginable. These novels read like long epistles, as if trekking the frame and run of an epistolary novel. But today, I remain content reading scripture. There are gardens mentioned in scripture too, within Ecclesiastes, Kings, Genesis, John.

What was it like, to bask in such a pristine bed of land—like a new forest, first breath of morning always? What was the color of nature like for you, Monet?

The world has become a vast terrain of every kind of letter, of accretions accruing toward a grand letter to what we've left behind, and are still enmeshed in.

This Anthropocene.

I chose a home that angled itself, the sun hitting the outer wall instead of shining into the inside. Inside, the day would burn up everything, scorch everything I hold dear. I have seen what heat and fire can do, make everything look old and used, discolored, weathered, worn down, undone.

To say one loves the Impressionists is to say one is dull, boring, too set in one's ways to embrace the novel of the fertile, to imagine a new world. Alas, this wandering lust, less wonderment, more desire turned greed, has turned the world in.

Your simpler days, Monet, seem so much more alluring. A charmed life, as it were. Your view seemed less cluttered, less noisy, less beat-up. You watched the light, its changing qualities from day to night, what happens to things with and against time. You depicted and celebrated the ordinary. Your view seemed closer to nature, what our own human nature is, after all, made of—by-and-by, for keeps, for good.

Tintinnabulation II

Tintinnabulation can be soft, also like memory
                              recaptured, a recapitulation.

Your voice, its first stirring, middle of morning.

God's voice, y'know—*when you hear it, you hear it.*

                                        You know it.

In Dejan Stojanovic's words:

                    "When the star dies, its eye closes;
                              tired of watching,
                    it flies back to its first bright dream."

I love Charles Simic too, that poem about newness,
                              this odd and rare age
    —nevermind the thesis, or observation disguised as precept.

Read the line about snow, and the impossibly black night.
Read about reading, to oneself, and aloud in a sitting room.
Read about dinner wine, red-faced drama:
                    the unfinished love poem.

        Because no one has really been forgiven,
        and this story needs to write its own ending
                    contingent on truth,
            the truth of thing and event and feeling

                              —and healing.

[If church bells are heard from afar, so far
they sound like an echo, that's the distant linger
                    and tremulous ring.]

Read the line about anger, then remorse over a mother's dying.

That was a line from another poet, crying into his metaphors.

Leavings for Poor Sojourners

"Do not forget, anyone who does not realize that he is
a child of God is unaware of the deepest truth about himself."

Saint Josemaría Escrivá

How the pews were wider, my legs
dangling over edge, slouched back

against hardwood oak, maybe maple.
Sit up straight, and my legs stretched

toward length of hymnals, gunmetal
gray, like tablets inscribed with holy

song—devotion now is awaiting noon
hour for the Angelus, or a series of

petitions. Or, to ask: When does prayer
become a poem, and a poem a prayer?

Oh Saint Monica, how you prayed.
Oh Saint Monica, how you waited.

Monica driving Augustine from table,
running after him to Rome; Monica

at one oratory after another, with bread
and porridge, no more wine in Milan.

Oh Saint Monica, replete with petition.
Know the poverty of riches, a willing

impoverishment, so the poor receive.
"For you are well aware of the grace of

our Lord Jesus Christ. Although he was
rich, he became poor for your sake so

that by his poverty you might become rich."
So goes 2 Corinthians 8:9 for the penitent.

Oh Saint Monica, in front of the bishop,
how fortuitous, again hearing his words:

"The child of those tears
shall never perish."

Rose Window, Baptistère Saint-Jean

"The sharp thorn often produces delicate roses."

Ovid

Saint Rose of Lima,
are you awake after your two hours of dream?

Saint Rose of Lima,
were your hands scalded, or burnt by candlelight?

Saint Rose of Lima,
what were your thoughts during daily Adoration?

Saint Rose of Lima,
what is it like to transcend the day, into the Perpetual?

Saint Rose of Lima,
shorn head, face chafed—what beauty, what burden?

Saint Rose of Lima,
wooden carving here, three roses like pink cameos.

Saint Rose of Lima,
crown of thorns worn tight, unseen, penance in secret.

Saint Rose of Lima,
in your given cloister—what did you choose to read?

Saint Rose of Lima,
in your given cloister—what hymns, what prayers?

Saint Rose of Lima,
in your given cloister—what did you see out the window?

Saint Rose of Lima,
patroness of embroiderers, look at my French scapular.

Saint Rose of Lima,
patroness of florists, look at my dried roses from church.

Saint Rose of Lima,
patroness of the pious, aggrieved by ridicule and unbelief.

Saint Rose of Lima,
patroness of the broken family, saddened by the world

—of wrong.

Blind Country of the Dying

"Death is no more than passing from one room into another.
But there's a difference for me, you know.
Because in that other room I shall be able to see."

Helen Keller

A hospital room is no home at all,
not one's bedroom. No gerbera daisy, red
in an emptied bottle, no such offered reprieve.
Nothing seems adequate as a salve or balm.
The posy of azaleas in hot pink—sudden
flare—like a crack in the dim light of the room.
The sound of the gray telly, wobbly
on a makeshift overhang, is muted.
Same message as my mother's door sign:
"Don't disturb. I'm already disturbed."
At 3.14am, someone posted a gif of a bison.
It was resting, heft of brown, wool mound on pasture.
Small goats hopped on its back, right up its head.
It dropped its head, heavy anchor, to the ground
as if to let it be known it was okay after all.
To become bed and playpen, involuntarily
someone else's amusement and brief joy.
This hospital bed could be this bison.
The potted white hydrangea is the baby goat—
where's the nanny, where's the billy goat?
Who is the chaperone tonight, who will stand in
as shepherd and brother, priest as good keeper?
I am as blind now, eyes closed, as I was enwombed,
entombed. This bed, how it cradles me, this chariot.
It carries me, like the long arms of an angel.
An angel will carry me to the hereafter, that's true.
Beside it, another angel who stood beside it
all those decades ago, I'll think when we meet again.
Again, I'll think it's okay to leave this world
behind; and behind it, every singular thing
I once thought precious but is no more mine.

Ecclesiastes 4:4

I.

I remember the windy day. An exceptional day for these parts. It gets rainy around here, and the rain is thick and heavy, as if the sky opened its stop gates, and sent in its floods. Some poet from London said she'd never seen rain like that. It was the first time she'd heard thunder. *I thought it was a bomb*, she said.

I'd only heard of thunder in school, in storybooks.

That's why we call them thunderstorms, I said.

I was so scared, she said.

It was so loud, I thought I was going to die.

II.

Death did have a sound as loud, as deafening.

But close to oneself.

Right in the ear.

As if only for your listening.

Only to show you the terror and ordeal of the punitive hereafter.

Of what temporal punishment left behind.

III.

Like an eternal tinnitus, I said. How deafness presents itself as excruciating sounds. A million macaques—shrill bark like the howling of the penitent.

It's not to be understood as an irony, I think to myself.

Purgatory could have that quality, that coming into being. The materiality of the unbearable-inescapable, if only for the thousand-to-two-thousand years. That's the going rate, that's what someone said. That's the right idiom to use, if one reads the idiom as an expression indigenous to the longsuffering [and it is the state of the longsuffering, and even that would be an arrant understatement]. Or something diagnostic, of an attribute almost, a mode of expression peculiar to its own music—of the cleansing fire.

IV.

That could be what the cleansing fire might feel like. At least the beginning of it, at least that's what I felt. At least, in my experience. Now, it seems right to speak of the personal, and the tentative, and the conditional, and the qualified. Only in an approximation, I think to myself, for what can a human being know of such things?

Cleansing fire on a windless, eternal day. That could be what might best express it, what it felt like, if only the words arranged themselves today, properly for this lyric that seems intent on description today. The presence-absence of soundlessness and sheer clamor. Convulsions of the vociferous, but for lack of any human words to say it like it is—always, always.

V.

Vexation: first heard years ago, uttered by second sister.

Vexation of the spirit, said with force, as scriptural import.

VI.

The New King James Version translates this as grasping for the wind.

The American Standard Version translates this as a striving after wind.

The Common English Bible with Apocrypha says this, too, is pointless.

Just wind chasing.

The Douay-Rheims Catholic Bible translates this as fruitless care.

VII.

Of the devout life,
>   what affections
>   and resolutions
> did Saint Francis de Sales speak of?

> In his sixth meditation,
> after our preparation and considerations,

>   how did he instruct us—

>   to feel
>   to think?

[...   ...   .   ]
[...   ...   .   ]

1. Tremble, my soul, at the thought.
> *O God,*
who will be my stay in that hour
when the pillars of the earth are shaken?

2. Abhor your sins, which alone can cause you
to be lost when that fearful day comes.
Surely I will judge myself now,
>   *that I be not judged;—*
I will examine my conscience,
>   *accuse, condemn, punish myself,*
that the Judge may not condemn me then.
>   *I will confess my faults,*
and follow the counsels given me.

[...   ...   .   ]
[...   ...   .   ]

Recompense for the Novelty of Gossip

Where is the silence of daybreak?

When is the rousing of consciousness,
the conscious self
                        as authorial
                        or intended
though no one speaks of such things these days.

These are dismal days,
                        sadfaced winkeys
                        ideogrammatic icons
                                        to signify
                        one glyph emotion after another.

These are the lost days of whispers.

[*Write about the woman's confession, and impending contrition.*]
[*Write about the priest, his indignation, and the telling penance.*]
[*Write about the sting of gossip.*]
[*Write about the silent scattering of feathers.*]
[*Write about the feather-strewn streets across town.*]
[*Write about the rampant, the irretrievable damage of feathers.*]
[*Write, then, about silence.*]
[*Write, then, about the inner begging for forgiveness.*]

Those are random thoughts, percolating, slow flow—
                        episodic memory,
                        semantic memory
                        in tow.

Father Jose Luis Lopez Carpio gave that homily
                        over a year ago;
            the women and men looked down
                        into their laps in shame,
                        clasped palms, anxious-nervous shuffle.

The surgeon has walked away for so long, no one can remember.

His head was down too.

How to unpack each moment
—narrative memory, then traumatic memory—
when one issues the other,
and what ensues is more talk, more mere talking about things?

Look, a meme about a donkey.

One donkey is sniffing at a fence picket, and says: "I love this post."

One meme tells you to just always pet a donkey—

whether you're mad,
whether you're sad.

Field Notes on the Flaming Heart

"Bring us rest. Guilt is fecund."

Frank Bidart

1.   Look at this bonfire room, emptied of occupants.
It's the same blank look—
             an acute, terrifying silence.
        Write a poem that has heart, you say.
That nobody desires to have anything to do with.
The space, and there is the covered grave,
already a vacuity where there was once giant emotion.

2.   After so many repetitions and ideological posturings,
             one turns back to just a few maxims.
The one about a building, like a clock tower or lighthouse,
the one with a hundred thousand million windows.
             The one about flux and no rule of conduct,
                our eternal motion.
Our constant becomingness, a situated dasein no less.

3.   The one about love as defined by language,
that even love is not spared the hazard
             and pickle of language.
The intricacies, the contusions. The knotty, unsettling strain.
That love may be but a deception, like the glow of fire.
The first tea rose like a bruising shade of pink,
        then this atomic orange, unpeeling its flames.
That just saying it makes it equally true.
The resonance, of rippling,
             like your deflected sound and tinted image.

4.   The anthropologist has scoured the terrain, its dry form
where nothing, like feeling, seems able to thrive.
             He is thinking what to scribe on a placard,
what nature of transcription to provide another precept.
In this land of deadening things, hastened into
          its own extremity, that margin also an expiration.

5.   Look at the heart of sudden grief.
There's no death,
and yet it is a death.
Someone died indeed—so goes the postmemory,
of how many lifetimes?
Yet, we meet every day, conscientiously,
at the turn of this fire-brick street, along the wide aisle
at every other store. Look at our collectibles-in-perpetuity,
our stash pulled out of drawers and luggage,
now stacked, tidy on a pyre.
We meet at the blaze and charring,
the flaming remnants and tall pipe of smoke.
We meet at the combustion, the engine red gone wrong.
We meet at the center of it all, the spectra of old illusions.
We meet at the small church, where every pew is full,
and you're ushered to two empty seats.
An early devotion within enclosed space.
A psalm and song. Another chorus, interred within a hymn.

6.   Look at the wildfire, how the imagery burns along with skin.
Look at the animal skin. Look at the thin skin,
of melon and apricot and tangerine,
of thinking otherwise.
This could have happened, this or that.
That this conversation—a long time in coming,
bittersweet as it was—could have been more ideal.
Like the one about life's afflictions,
how hard the bad fortune, the soreness and danger.
How romantic, one thinks, how thoroughly thought-through.
As if rigor or an equation or fuel could circumvent tragedy.

7.   The anthropologist is by himself, in the cavern of lost things,
gigantic hole carved out of mountainside.
It houses a pond that dips innocuously,
narrow cylinder diving down a vertical tunnel,
then a sprawling lattice of deep underwater caves.
The cavern has been given its own name:
Saint Maron's Grotto of Volitional Isolation.

8.   There is no silencing the emotion or the journey.
No cushioning or sublime math
or padded walls to hurl oneself against.

No couch deep enough to sink into. No bed warm enough,
                                        without you in it.
No heart big enough, or skin thick enough.
Look at the water you speak of, its black depth,
and how we'll both drown in it.
                        Look at our heads
                        beneath water.

9.   Our limbs flailing in the air, the sky already incandescent.
        Above us, the scorching of our best days, coals and glint in air.
        Our mouths forced open, agape and taking in water,
                        so our sounds dissolve, dissipate.
                        And along with the sounds,
        the regrettable feeling of what it means to suffer loss.
        This is not a heartbreak poem, you say—
                        or deep cuts and sudden fracture.
        This is a moment of penance, its own sea of flame.
        With you dead, almost a decade now, oh grand love of my life.
        With you dead—
                        here I am,
                        still wondering what might have been.

10.   Where is the tall structure, the imposing one you spoke of?
                        After last pulse, and rattle of death.
        Where is the far shore for you to wave from,
        from which you promised to smile your big smile,
                        and say you're okay, you've arrived?
        The barn has turned a drab and darkened red,
                                like spilled blood,
        as has our bell tower, our chapel, our pavements
                                to the secret cloister.
        This might as well be a heartbreak poem:
                                who cares,
                        and who has seen your epitaph?
        This, a eulogy and an atonement,
                        for not having known better,
        or expected more. For not having loved truly—

                                or ever been
                                happy enough.

Dear Blue-Eyed Cat

Scene 1

This was supposed to be a Dear John letter. But now, it might as well be written up to Maudie. Look at the kitsch of the poster, the rough-drawn title like a cheap font. *There is no universally beautiful typeface*, you say. Every word or phrase will find its shape; the lengths and curves have to fall into place.

[Saint Gertrude remembers growing up.]
[Saint Gertrude was the smallest of her siblings.]

You say *we can read a novel in sans serif*, and we agree to disagree. Just like the half-drawn canary Maudie has painted into the corner. *Without its beak, it must be a fairy*, Everett says. He insists he's in charge of things—the house, the dogs, the poultry, the one she hacks up for dinner, the fish for delivery, the huge wheelbarrow, the new truck, the signage he removes from the road upon Maudie's death.

Scene 2

[Saint Gertrude didn't think marriage was for her.]
[Saint Gertrude didn't want an arranged marriage.]

Everett is in charge. He turns over to face Maudie's back, and slips his arm around her waist to touch her breast. He brings his hand down to lift her nightshirt. Everett is in charge; no gruffness or orphan past can blanket desire. No bottle or shroud, no concealment.

[Saint Gertrude remembers the call to prayer and contemplation.]

Scene 3

[Saint Gertrude is safe in the monastery of her own formation.]

In one scene, Everett hits Maudie on the face, with the back of his hand. Such force, you notice, something that could fracture bone and face. How then can you—yes, you, gazing into the same mirror—see goodness in this man?

This man is called Everett, but it might as well be that man, or you, walking down the street. How do we fall in love with such flawed character? What a great smallness Maudie's happiness is. What a simple shape, like a square with perfect right angles.

[Saint Gertrude is safe in the monastery of her own building.]

Scene 4

The wooden frame is painted a cool white, only one coat so the grain shows through. Its own patterns like painted lines. It seems a whole life can be already, preternaturally, framed—or it can frame itself, with a kind of volition.

Saint Gertrude of Nivelles is seated on the square cushion brought to this floor. I am at the Chapel of The Incarnation, where I am kneeling, forehead to ground, and she is there beside me, like a friend. It is just before seven in the evening. There is so much peace here, our Church of Saints Peter and Paul.

Today is the Feast of Saints Peter and Paul, how timely. It didn't occur to me, but here I am. One gets used to the way small miracles happen. That's the way of the pious and prayerful. That's business as usual for the believer.

[Saint Gertrude is praying, just as I am.]

Scene 5

Maudie's choice to stay was the remarkable decision—a deliverance, if you'd like, for both the artist and lover, patron and muse. There's a beauty in such steadfast behavior, like the white cat in her painting. It is plush with wide cheeks and body. It has fur—you see it ruffled, the edges—but no detailing, no lines are drawn in.

This has become a Dear Saint Gertrude letter. The cat has blue eyes; they reach out to you. They're two opals, stark like oval ponds. There is largely the thinness of white. White, like a slope of first snow. White like crumpled satin, down the length of a forgotten dress.

Scene of Saint Martin:
Monostich Catalog

Saint Martin curled up in a ball, cereal box of new cat house.

+ + +

Roll, belly up—bared. Surface scent, marked territory.

+ + +

No response to my voice. Asleep on bed of holy cards.

+ + +

Saint Modestos of Jerusalem and Saint Julian of Norwich.

+ + +

Saint Jerome's lion chewing on his slippers, old monastery.

+ + +

Of new cat house. Saint Jerome, according to Vincenzo Catena.

+ + +

Where is the removed thorn? In the jar; is it under the candlestick?

+ + +

Saint Martin over keyboard—look up at typing hands, in surrender.

+ + +

Saint Martin de Porres with his cat. Over the same, shared plate.

Necessity 101

[N is for the nice neighbor.]

[N is for the notion of the good life.]
[N is for the notion of the good life in a dense city.]
[N is for the notion of life made good on an island.]

[N is for neighborliness as a necessity.]

Like an expressed need, I said. *Like clean air*, you said. *Clean streets, clean corridors.* These weekends, it's tidewrack, as we sweep the beach.

The way small things matter, Ashbery wrote. The way a viable future may be brokered. The way all of us have a kind and gentle side to us. That side of nature that is humane.

[N is for that notion of nobleness in the kind act.]

Proverbs 19:17— *Whoever is kind to the poor lends to the Lord*
who will recompense him for his kindness.

Saint Gertrude needs cat-sitting, you said. *Could you please?* House-sitting with Saint Gertrude, who cuddles up to the homeless.

Make sure we always have enough, we agreed. *Enough two-dollar bills for every rough sleeper.* Saint Gertrude has an old cat bed at the night shelter too, next to the rough sleepers.

Consider it a staycation, I said. *Bring you a good book to read*, you said. *There's no need*, I said, *Saint Gertrude of Nivelles is reward enough.*

Really?

Really. Really. Saint Gertrude of Nivelles, the patron saint we cat lovers just love. Saint Gertrude of Nivelles, patron saint of all cats.

[N is for the underrated notion of niceness.]

Niceties are easy when you think of them as necessary.

Dear Saint Matilda—
The Slight Evidence of Epistolary Autofiction
Today, or Some Day Years Ago

"For me, prayer is a burst from my heart,
it is a simple glance thrown toward heaven,
a cry of thanksgiving and love
in times of trial as well as in times of joy."

Saint Thérèse of Lisieux, *Story of a Soul*

This was supposed to be a Dear John letter. This was supposed to be so many other things, as so many other things—of the past, of long-ago autobiographical memory—seem to be nowadays.

This was also supposed to be a crack, a flash of fiction. Like postcard fiction, maybe even actually written up on a postcard, as if the media one worked in did suddenly seem to matter more today. As if textuality did arrange its being around such surrounding condition, like old environment, like some singular stratum of rock, and how you study it for what it has trapped through the ages, for what it has to say.

As if, what my teacher once underlined, the only thing he underlined for many pages. As if it was the two-worded phrase that only seemed to matter. With that, he said, I could write anything I wanted. That moment, his sliver of a line—that thin shaft, also a crack and flash—took on something of a hint of light, itself glinting against what it surfaced.

The surface too, the surface it stood on, and believed in.

What surfaces do our beliefs rest themselves on, and what relationships exist between them? Between one belief and the next, one belief and the other. Between text and text, text and surface, surface and surface. What relations, what precise quality or nature or place of meaning? Even as each meaning rests against another, the same going for all meaning, even that.

Even as. *Even as*, that's the new inscription, the new phrase of choice and purchase.

As in the moment of this moment, this breath, halted to underscore the moment.

To turn into an accent, like another slight curve turning upward, toward the light. To breathe, to write with a gaze so directed. Heavenward, that's the word my godfather used. What does it mean now, that all the words—all my words—have taken on this singular importance, this assignment of place and destination?

Not a finger pointing at the moon, like in the old days. But the moon is also place and situation and hope and such quiet displacement of mood. But also region of mood, as if to stow or prop, to lay bare. Not an insistence, but a broaching. An approaching. Not of a proposition, but a gesture like a trace or a hint again, or a whisper.

But the moon is also stratum, one of many settings like a station, a sudden recurring word I like these days. These days like these moments like these scenes like these small breaths.

Like a seating of things and feelings. Like a chair. This chair, and no other. Set down, in its position, to position these things, and more words. And more moments, Saint Matilda.

Saint Matilda, the Quedlinburg *Itala* fragment at rest, housed for so long at home. At home in Quedlinburg Abbey, the oldest extant illustrated biblical manuscript. The Book of Samuel, its first part, portion—as if apportioned and in proportion. Look at the old drawings, encased in equal boxes. This, narrative too. Graphic novel, fifth century. More frames of more tellings, before the calligraphic flourish, more of the slight curvature looking to the light.

Heavenward. Mind and heart pointing, that's the only gesture of origin.

These days, and sudden mornings. Of station. Of place and belonging. One location, one more situation. One singular situation. One more position my words find themselves comfortable in.

As if. *As if*—that is, to bring close to the surface. To come close enough, so one can breathe in the shared moment, the air between things, between you and me, and what surrounds. Shared air, and all the sound that has gone out the room. Its silence, the same silence the contemplatives have been speaking about. Through more texts, more of the textuality that doesn't speak of oldness or newness, not these days at least. Dear Saint Matilda, what will I make of all this, all these written surfaces?

What of classical narratology, how fractured it now looks, how dramatically rent? And what is left is one cleft after another, here and there, even as one notices the cleaving, in both senses of the word. No violence, even as one perceives the coming together of things, alongside the soft estrangement of things. What helps us stick, stitch these things together? And what presents itself split open, another chance moment for healing? Not estrangement, it seems more now than ever—not that violence either—but more of two strangers looking at one another through both window and mirror. The strangeness of encounter, that's the nature of narratological motion here. As much presence, as much motion as emotion.

This was supposed to be a story about a blue-eyed cat. Or was it *the* blue-eyed cat? The Blue-Eyed Cat, capitalized as if it needed to underscore its title as presence.

This was supposed to be a Dear John letter, it said so long ago.

It was that long ago.

What of point of view, the kind that persists, even as it transposes, transports? What of the perspectives that carry with them all manner of scene and story? What of focalization, what narrative detail makes it through, what gets left behind? Not forgotten, but kept absent, yet close. Close to the heart until the availing of its moment, its movement of emotion. And then, some gaining momentum; and sometimes, the occasion and measure of metaphor.

How many characters have come and gone? How many narrators, how many of their shifting perspectives? What of subjectivity, as it pushes through one limit after another, the limits stacked so closely in the mind? And within the heart, when one realizes the closeness, the connectedness of things, between here and there, you and I, always. Over and over again.

This was supposed to be a Dear John letter, so it said, yes it said once. And only once, you and I remember. Who are the you and I, who remains of the you and I in these things said? And what of the unsaid, something I used to like to say as well, over and over again.

Saying and unsaying.

The saying and unsaying—what measure of things, the narrator asks?

This was supposed to be an epistolary something.

But now, it might as well be written up to Maudie—again, Maudie for Maud Lewis, as portrayed by Sally Hawkins. Maudie, the term of endearment for the Nova Scotia folk artist.

Did I say the cat had blue eyes, the kind of blue I now remember encountering twenty years ago? It has been that long a time of separation, hasn't it?

What did Francis Avenue look like then, and what does it look like now?

The blue was something between sky and stone, teal as the sea.

The blue would glisten, lapis glints, like sunlight in his eyes.

> Like bright sapphire,
> across white waves.

Down the same lengths of a forgotten memory, Dear Saint Matilda.

> And more moments, Saint Matilda.

Thank you for this moment, Saint Matilda.

> Dear Saint Matilda.

> Dear Saint Matilda—

> Dear Saint Matilda,

The Contingency of Saying

If I say *I love you.*
If I say *this love we share will be our last.*
If I say *we should trust our every emotion.*

That even at their darkest, they reify the same.

The same culling of past acts of love, of endearment.

That's what the novel was, haven't you known all along?

[*In the anachrony, where do the analepsis and prolepsis begin?*]
[*Someone mentioned metalepsis, an intrusion of the extradiegetic?*]
                    [*Or rather, an intervention or mediation,*
                                something tender.]
[*Who could share in this ontological movement?*]
[*Who might understand its kindness, no kindling of a fiction?*]

[*The tellability of qualia—*
            what coda of the felt, of the experiential?]
[*Every moment floats coda. Adrift, like an extension of a long beacon.*]
[*Of light, its duration*
        through the resonant pause
                        and stretch of scene.]
[*Of the silence, as I keep saying—even within gap, across lacunae.*]
[*Of the utterance. The idea of deixis—*
            who is speaking then,
            and when, where?]

A book of letters, each epistle like a gift of the holy angels.

If I say *you should stay.*
If I say *this staying will be forever.*
If I say *every decision arrives at the same decision.*

That as you confessed: *you are, as I am.*

You are, as I am content in this mirror of things.
All things now made for this, to house our love.

Eternal Motion

After David Medalla's Cloud Gates

There is no redundancy here.
There is no superfluity, even in life's assessment.

No one's looking.
No one, Oh Ephemerae of Dissolutions.
No one is there, in the room where it all happened.
So long ago, the haptic memory has become a fiction.
The visual-spatial—the sense of a place,
                              location
                                        of the self
                              under such strangeness.

The room seems like a fiction, but it is real.
You know it is real, its squarish angularity.
I know it is real, the way you hold my hand.

        [*The repetitions are eternal,*
                        seeming inversions.]
        [*Repetitions. Relentless, unremittingly so.*]
        [*Of perpetual, sustained circumvolutions.*]

                        [*For forever—really?*]

Of an extended metaphor extending itself,
series of infolding turns, so much as to disappear.
No lodged positions, no milky consistency.
The resulting invisibility, also a contingent condition.

It is there, it exists like this colored sky.

        No one's looking,
        but there's our seat—

                        ensconced.

DAILY
EXAMEN

ACT II
SCENES I-XIII

Conversation on Mount Olivet

This is Kidron Valley, something you never knew back then. What is it like to stand on old ground, and not know its history, the gravity of everything that has happened on the land, under the same sky?

You know where it begins, from where you now stand. You've walked around the Armenian Quarter, and reached the Christian Quarter. And here, from the Old City of Jerusalem, there it is—just right of the far north—one beginning amidst so many of these scriptural beginnings.

[Where should I begin reading today?]

[Which psalm, which parable, which wisdom line?]

The old man in the shop is saddened. He is speaking of better days. His lament—that many who live by love have long gone, no matter how hard it is to leave home, this Holy Land.

[" The Christian desires the way of love,"
the old man said,
with tears in his eyes.]

"The way of peace," the old man said, as he looks at you like a long-lost son. He is gazing upon foreignness, but never acknowledges it.

He only sees sameness.

In our lifelong searching.
In our thirst for faithfulness.

[I remember the Armenian seminarian in Pasadena—was he a sub-Diaconate or full Deacon? What was his discernment process like? Of the handful of callings, which was the most forceful, almost deafening?]

His son is shuffling behind the counter, placing crosses in trays and boxes. These are sterling silver, beautifully made by hand. He points to the ones with the Christ figure, and says to take one of those. The crucifixes are the most striking—elaborate detailing, precise.

"Eyes on Christ always," he insists.

Eyes on Christ always.

Beyond these heavyset walls and watchtowers, how far more to the Dead Sea?

Which gate will you start and end your journey on, now that you've touched the stone at Damascus Gate and Herod's Gate, then Zion Gate?

You take that right-angled turn, and walk out into the sun. This is Jaffa Gate, leading out into Jaffa Road, following so many pilgrims' footsteps to the port.

The port of Jaffa—
who sees Jonah pushing off from the pier?

Into the belly of the whale,
who is set to the test, only to return to shore?

There is the history of a postern gate at another doorway.

Now,
the penitent have found their way here,
how they have made their passage home—
how many have come and gone.

Soft bidding, these openings
of egress and entrance.

At New Gate, you stand beneath its distinct arch of uneven stone. At this high point, the air is fresher, like a cool mint.

And you head back from where you came, into the Christian Quarter.

Saint Josemaría Escrivá's Donkey Theology

"Oh blessed perseverance of the donkey that turns the water-wheel!
Always the same pace. Always the same circles. One day after another:
everyday the same. Without that, there would be no ripeness in the fruit,
nor blossom in the orchard, nor scent of flowers in the garden.
Carry this thought to your interior life."

Saint Josemaría Escrivá, *The Way*

What now?

There, now…

There, there…

To suffer no fools—that sort of early puzzlement.

For years, the statement seemed too thick, or obfuscating even.

Like donkey theology, that donkeys have theology.

When one puts it like this, someone balks.

Note to Lenten self:
That was then. This is now.

[*Self says Lenten practice will be different this year.*]

When someone statuesque
like Saint Josemaría Escrivá puts it like that—

this, then, becomes the *theology of the donkey.*

Here goes the nothing
that came before
an everything,
how it's all settled

like nature
into
the only things
that matter to me

now.

[Start idioms with the word "now", the litany of.]

[Can litany be used like this, so perfunctory?]

[Where is the world stripped of sacred meaning?]

[Which aching moments, of our small, dismal worlds?]

"And what is the secret of perseverance?"

Saint Josemaría Escrivá asks
of himself,
then us—

upon rereading
and encounter.

[Which same circles and same paces to draw upon?]

[Which carried thoughts now, for this interior life?]

"Love."
"Fall in Love—"

Saint Josemaría Escrivá writes,
for himself
and the lover and beloved
in you.

"Fall in Love, and you will not leave him."

Jerusalem Donkey Waiting
for the Shadow of the Cross

"As they approached Jerusalem and came to Bethphage
on the Mount of Olives, Jesus sent two disciples, saying to them,
'Go to the village ahead of you, and at once you will find a donkey
tied there, with her colt by her. Untie them and bring them to me.'"

Matthew 21:1–2

Where is the edge of the ocean
but the edge of the ocean?

Where is the edge of the song—
                    where,
                        its beginning and ending?

                        Song edge,
                        outer and inner limits.

                        To swim.

                        Along, and against.

                        Through, and toward.

                        From within and without, considering.

Look at the cross on every donkey's back,
rising like emblazoned shadow, burnt fur
                        a darkened wenge or walnut.

Liminality can be a branding too,
hot iron the length of human back, shoulder to shoulder.

Look at the pick-axe, you say,
quiet and non-descript like a tau cross.

It's the same one in the monastery,
nailed to the wall in four places.

Mangy Donkey Sestina:
A Triptych Dismantled & Reconstituted

"Rejoice greatly, O daughter Zion!
  Shout aloud, O daughter Jerusalem!
Lo, your king comes to you;
  triumphant and victorious is he,
humble and riding on a donkey,
  on a colt, the foal of a donkey."

Zechariah 9:9

look, donkey
crossbanding
how far a journey
crosshatching
mercy
then crossbearing

into more crossbearing
again donkey
again mercy
crossbanding
crosshatching
another journey

another journey
crossbearing
crosshatching
where now, donkey
which crossbanding
for love of mercy

for love of mercy
and journey
crossbanding
crossbearing
forever donkey
forever crosshatching

forever crosshatching
mercy mercy mercy
upon holy donkey
upon journey
always crossbearing
always crossbanding

always crossbanding
forever crosshatching
forever crossbearing
holy holy holy mercy
holy holy holy journey
holy holy holy donkey

crossbanding mercy
crosshatching journey
crossbearing donkey

Vista // Vision // Visitation

"… one Godsend after another, the only way to apprehend these accounts …"

"… was I the only one who saw the old man …"

"… at the Church of Saint Anne, was I the only one to see …"

"… after the crowd thinned into an empty atrium, sea of stone …"

"… as spacious as the saxe sky in Coccorante's painting …"

"… Veronese's Jesus is haloed, against the gray column; he leans forward …"

"… Jesus is pointing at the paralytic, his pleading gaze for healing …"

"… the paralytic's face clear in Murillo, Jesus adorned in royal purple …"

"… from which perspective does one view each painting, and the history …"

"… where does one position oneself, under which of the five porticoes …"

"… do you remember the shrubbery, the brightness of day, yet cool air …"

"… do I/you remember the old man looking at us, from afar …"

"… do I/you remember looking around to see who he was beckoning …"

"… do I/you remember looking back, only to see him gone … impossible …"

"… only to see him on the stone stairs, even farther down the vista …"

"… do I/you remember the smile, warm welcome, of a foster father …"

"… at the Church of Saint Anne, near where the Virgin Mary grew up …"

"… the Church of Saint Anne survived the conquest of Jerusalem …"

"… how it changed hands, and fell to Napoleon III as a gift …"

"… how it was an architect, Christophe-Edouard Mauss, who unearthed the Pool …"

"… was I the only one who saw the old man at the Church of Saint Anne …"

"… was he Saint Joachim, father of Mary, mother of Jesus, mother of God …"

"… was he the paralytic, beaming because he could walk again, on his own …"

"… was he the other old man I saw down the stone steps at the Tomb of the Prophets …"

"… was he Jeremiah, who stayed by my side as I wept …"

"… was he Saint Augustine, who knew how much I needed to know, unknow …"

"… was he Saint Anthony of Padua, even before I knew how lost I was …"

"… was he Saint Jude Thaddeus, even before I knew of praying for the lost cause …"

"… was he Saint Joseph, foster father of Jesus, patron of the dying …"

"… maybe he was Saint Joseph, Protector of Holy Church …"

"… maybe he was Saint Francis Xavier, whose tomb I prayed at …"

"… maybe he was Saint Francis Xavier, whose name I took …"

"… was I the only one who saw the old man …"

"… was he the old man I saw in my dream in my twenties …"

"… was he the old man I saw in my dream in my mid-thirties …"

"… was he the old man I saw in my dream, again, in my forties …"

"… was I the only one who saw the old man …"

"… the old man had so many words, so many words … the words, all his words …"

"… the old man's words, mouthed, full and emphatic, yet in silence …"

"… the burning words, bright and afire, yet unseen, if only I/you knew …"

"… was I the only one who saw the old man …"

"… was I the only one who saw the old man at the Church of Saint Anne …"

What I Saw at the Church of the Sepulchre of Saint Mary: Scene XVIII

"Do you want to be daring in a holy way, so that God may act through you? Have recourse to Mary, and she will accompany you along the path of humility, so that, when faced by what to the human mind is impossible, you may be able to answer with a *fiat!*—be it done!, which unites the earth to Heaven."

Saint Josemaría Escrivá, *Furrow*

00:02:34 Speaker 1

How many steps were there?

[They were grand, this is what I remember.]
[The walk down into the mouth of a magnificent sanctuary.]
[Did I know then of what a safe space looked like?]
[Did I know such sanctity of the rarefied, sacred space?]
[None of the artifice of our own complex constructions.]
[None of the tangled fabrications of curated time and space.]
[Here, I find peace—and belonging, in the midst of strangers.]
[This is what it's like to belong, in a country of strange faces.]

00:02:36 Speaker 1

Going down.

[There were forty-seven steps, now that I know this.]
[There are forty-seven steps, now that I say and know this.]
[In this treatise, the past and present seem indistinguishable.]
[What is tense, when all you know these days is the Glory Be?]
[Glory be to the Father, and to the Son, and to the Holy Spirit.]
[As it was in the beginning, is now, and ever shall be. Amen.]
[Amen, Amen—another iteration forever, and more, and more.]
[This is the treatise, of new beginnings, going forward.]

[This treatise of lyric tracts, now that you read it, think of it.]
[Now when you see it, feel it, write it, one line to the next.]

[These are not the details you attend to in the face of grandeur.]
[This holy space, its innumerable beauties, its every blessing.]
[This is what it's like to be moved by the same purpose.]
[The longing of the pilgrim, moving in one direction.]
[You don't know you're walking into your own death.]
[You don't know—this enduring death, persistent dying to self.]
[You don't know what awaits the wonder, this miracle of days.]
[You don't know the joy—work sanctified, sanctified life.]
[The direction toward love, our eternal love for God.]

The One Happy Thing

"It is a happy thing that there is no royal road to poetry."

Gerard Manley Hopkins

No poet in this country cares for Hopkins,
a faraway poet said.

But for the sense of the utopian ideal
in his *Heaven-Haven*.

But for such an imagined *good* place—
was it also an epoch, some temporal state

of mind, the psychology of the moment? Then
emotion more like a fleeting feeling,
                        then fleet
of more of the same.

        Like holy love, heaven-sent.

On feast days, beyond holy days of obligation.

On Sundays, which are always feast days,
                       didn't we know?

An accent on its significance, without ambiguity
like a renewal of vows, forcefulness.

                Sacrosanctum Concilium, no. 106

Therein a gift of the Second Vatican Council:

        "Hence the Lord's day is the original feast day."

That was, *is*—will always be—poetry.

That statement of truth, reclaimed like an eternal ictus.

A fit of awakened memory—
                always iconic first
                then echoic—
                seizure, hint,
                                sometimes admonition,
                and always, expressed intimation
                for all.

            As perceptual as it is procedural.
            As implicit and prospective,
                            as it is declarative.

    Then, flight, as I said once,
                            again.

    Then, church bells, once
    and for all—*thereto,*

                thereof, therewith, thereunder—
                                their distant pealing
            far-flung
                                faraway

                        far-off belfry

                    [...   ...   .   ]
                    [...   ...   .   ]

                note bene,
                the notations
                        imprint
                themselves

                                    thereupon

                    this *good* place
                    this sensible world

                    of head
                    of heart.

The Tallest Speech Act of All

I own the sun, the moon, the stars—the ones
that appear in love songs, those I own too.

[*I don't own anything of this world.*]

Who is the speaker of this poem?

Who is the speaker of the poem you're reading?

Who is the speaker of any poem?

That's the first question Cornelius Eady asks.

> Of a poem,
> as if the poem would deliver
> an answer,
> define its own myriad voices,
> claim some ontological presence.

> Who is the speaker
> —within a defamiliarized thought,
> that luminosity—
> for a mystic?

A God poem must reference a precision,
its own certitude of intent.

A humbling of the poet's mind and practice—
one's spirit
in attending to language
and all things.

The transcendental signified is situated, proper.

It knows itself, knows who it is, who exists in the utterance.

It speaks with that kind of unstrained clarity.

Knowingness, Signs, Professions

I.

Prophecy. There is the notion of prophecy, an originary openness of meaning that defers its imparted meaning. Till time arrives. The arrival of time, as important as the meaning and its eventual unfolding.

II.

Like a paper tiger or crane or sparrow. I thought of the sparrow, despite its stark sound, that jarring sound. I remember how boxy the paper sparrow looked, how inelegant; yet, a done thing. How some things, I wonder, are made to be what they've become—it'd be easy to say *for better or worse*, but there's no for better or worse in this. The paper sparrow looked like it belonged, near earth, close to the ground on which is walked its small form. As if flinching from flight, something it could—and already knew how to—do. But paper boat, I think and now say. Because it's what I first came to notice, and in a way, came to know.

Because the paper boat came right after the paper box, and the child noticed how two or more things could be made out of one sheet of paper. A sheet of white paper, one side sliced off, to make for a perfect square. The folded lines arranging themselves, like a map of what was, of what it took.

III.

What miracles—the miracle of joy—did Saint Joseph witness in the Child Jesus? A jubilant Simeon, Baby Jesus cradled in arm, declaring Christ "a light for revelation to the Gentiles". As in Luke 2:32. Then, this evening's Compline, the *Nunc dimittis*. In Latin, restated in your head in English.

As affirming a canticle, the echo. An echo across the ages, for all the ages.

Already, the Magi showed up, across vast lands. For worship. They showed up as "first-fruits of the Gentiles". As vouched for, Saint Thomas

Aquinas over his desk and papers. Then, the myrrh as foreshadowing of the mortal death to come. Then, the gold for a king already here. Then, the frankincense—high offering, sweet scent carried aloft—only for Christ Jesus, true God and true man. Inseparably.

IV.

"Fully man and fully God," the priest says. As in Hypostatic union.

As in affirming the Christology.

Never Gnostic Docetism. Nor the Monophysites, or Nestorian heresy.

> How the proclamation has endured.

> Through the Council of Nicaea.
> Through the Council of Ephesus.
> Through the Council of Chalcedon.
> Through the Council of Constantinople.

V.

Prophecy. The real eventuality of timed meaning. Unexpected, unexceptional until the epiphany. Of a truth unfurled. An unveiling, outspread.

Truth beyond time, beyond the here and now.

That's another kind of transcendence.

> Another climb,
> another elevation.

Lazarus the Friend of Christ:
Larnaca Tomb Inscription

"Our friend Lazarus has fallen asleep, but I am going there to awaken him."

John 11:11

It is said that Saint Lazarus never smiled after.

After being
raised from the dead—

+

What was Bethany like,
mouth of the tomb agape
in a long yawn?

How many people arrived as witness?

[Was the linen cloth—like old habits dying
hard, oh Mary Undoer of Knots—
unwrapped or pulled off,
in leavings, our old remains both material and not?]

+

This is all germane matter, on the dotted nose.

What do they say,
about cutting off your nose,
only to spite the face?

What do they say about our open wounds
of overlong wrongdoing
one offense after another
against reason and truth,
against right conscience?

+

[Reading scripture brings out the proverbial,
         and life reads itself into the idiomatic,
               —timely, versified.]

+

So, this is what awe and hope look like,
         their faces as ashen?

So, this is what unbelief looks like, also?

+

How does the Johannine Gospel read now,
the account where even death doesn't have the last word?

Where does language go beyond each epoch—
        the words, how they thread
        across the plains and more language?

        Lost
             in time,
        then unearthed

        into the soft light
        of day and all who arrived

                to see.

Christ's Tear for Lazarus:
Abbey of la Trinité, Vendôme

"Did I not tell you that if you have faith you will see the glory of God?"

John 11:40

Look at the mosaic of Mary, Martha and Lazarus.

How they arranged themselves
into this exact pattern of things,
Cesare Vagarini's eye
recalling Florence, Milan, Tuscany.

What is Al-Eizariya like,
this town called "the place of Lazarus"?

+

If you only knew what I saw—

If only I could show you the faces—

If only you saw for yourself—

The look of eternal death,
the howl and wail
ever-plaintive,
lingering whimper
for all time.

No echo in this void
of the forgotten.

+

Of the devout life,
what choice did Saint Francis de Sales speak of?

In his ninth meditation,
after our preparation and considerations,

what choice
did he point to?

O Hell, I abhor thee now and for ever;
I abhor thy griefs and torments, thine endless misery,
the unceasing blasphemies and maledictions
which thou pourest out upon my God;—
and turning to thee, O blessed Paradise, eternal glory,
unfading happiness, I choose thee for ever as my abode,
thy glorious mansions, thy precious and abiding tabernacles.

O my God, I bless Thy Mercy which gives me the power
to choose—O Jesus, Saviour, I accept Thine Eternal Love,
and praise Thee for the promise Thou hast given me
of a place prepared for me in that blessed New Jerusalem,
where I shall love and bless Thee for ever.

+

If only you saw the endless sea

of lost souls—

they stretch
like their weeping
into eternal darkness.

+

You wouldn't have cause to smile too.

+

You would have wept for all those years too.

[*Was it seventy years,*
or was it

seven hundred?]

+

Thereafter,

      back here
      in the world of the living,

      you would have wept
      for another twelve years.

          You would have
                wept
         like so, too.

The Cross of Hope:
View From Church of Agios Lazaros

"Jesus said to her, 'I am the resurrection and the life. The one who believes in me will live, even though they die; and whoever lives by believing in me will never die. Do you believe this?'"

John 11:25–26

[*And now, it's come to this.*]

Perhaps the clay from the other poems
is the pantile now, more material remains of old.

    More object of consideration—
    what began as inspection,
    then attention,
    and now meditation of the abstract

        like this prompt
        weighting of thought.

Perhaps the churchyard lent its dry stone—
        now the weighing again,
        heavy measure of study
            here and there
            but bluntness,
      this rugged rubble
      against dressed-up ashlar.

+

Is our conversation sandstone today,
        or is it limestone?

        Granite, or basalt?

Is the basalt on you
—the slab tucked under—
a dark gray,
or glassy?

Both
forthwith
your eyes.

Is the wetness
distress or regret?

[Oh, Our Lady
of Sorrows,
please pray for us.]

+

Let it be relief.

Let it be the suddenness
invariably—
of succor then.

+

He reads John 11:9–10—

Jesus answered,

"Are there not twelve hours of daylight?
If someone walks in the daylight,
he does not stumble,
because he sees by the light of this world.
But if he walks at night,
he stumbles,
because he does not have the light."

+

Who is he who reads at the lectern today?

Who is walking through these scriptural readings,
                    then yearend homily;
                who then recites the Creed by heart?

                                [*From the heart.*]

Who is sitting beside me today, is it you as stranger or friend?

            Are you a friend of Christ on occasion,
                                or for keeps
                        and the eternal good?

+

Someone is reading aloud from his seat—

                "See how he loved him!"

+

            [*And now, how it's come to this.*]

Perhaps the villages I speak of in poems—

Perhaps the villages I variously walked, and now see again—

Perhaps the villages are poems,
                    and the poems now
                            and again,
                the same villages—

Perhaps the weeping villages are the feast-day poems.

There are, after all, villages that reach back
                                into origins,
                        like I said,
                        like the moment

                        we decidedly
                                agreed to agree.

Reading Poetry
in St Lazarus Church, Yangon

"Because my name is Lazarus, and I live."

G. K. Chesterton

They say converts are the most ardent.

They say their fire is Yosemite's firefall—
fall of water welling,
lava river.

They say their fire is lucid crystal,
firefly spectacle
of that Nagoya forest.

They say their fire is like parhelia.

Halo, refracted light
from the sun,
aureate crown over horizon.

The horizon is as unchanging
as the ternary pageant
of orbs
lamps on one lampstand
this life-giving light,
we speak of plainly.

Look at this diorama meant for us—

Paired acreage
of light
like Moses and Elijah, flanking.

But how
    the Transfigured Christ
            shines
        resplendent,
        radiant glare.

    Oh Risen Christ,
    Sun Pillar to the World.

In the atmosphere of the clouds,
    you see no illusion
        but a mirror
  of what faith can become.

Leading light.

A keen light guide,
itself lensing.

DAILY
EXAMEN

***

ACT III
SCENES I-XIX

Fr Gabriel's Oboe

I.

A song, the sacred sound of sanctified *sound*.

Question: Can a song—without lyric, without words—be a prayer?

Response: A song is language too.

Response: Its own language, music as being, its own givenness.

Response: Sound is language is text is (*when sacrosanct*) prayer.

That qualification came from virtue,
                    from God-fear turned God-love.

II.

Gabriel's Oboe, in any form,
no matter the player or instrument or how big the orchestral sound,
is the song of the angels.

III.

It is early morning, and dawn's light is angel song too.

The light enters my window, just as the outside lights up.

There is no delayed conveyance.

                    No jammed carriage.

Yet with the flute and oboe, you can discern—
                    this is the distinction
                    of what it truly means
                                        to discern—
the empyrean passage, aerial,
its own settled firmament.

IV.

The wild blue yonder:
a cliché so sublime, it doesn't lose its newness, of character.

V.

Fr Gabriel tires easily these days, has to lean
into each act of contrition—true and sincere contrition,
                              no compunction.

By definition, compunction is fleeting, mere feeling.

An *autem prickear*, now obsolete
                —perhaps it was ill-timed, ill-suited,
                              now indecorous?—
is nowhere and anywhere because the language
has fallen into disuse;
                as is the current sense of things,
                        of departure,
                              the sadness of disaffection.

An abrupt prick of the conscience—pointed, apical,
                              barbed thorn wreath.

VI.

Craig Hella Johnson has dramatic hands.

Even hymns have some fixed order, strict metric patterning.
Hymns, and what employed articles of meaning.

                Read: the anaphora and paradox.
                Read: the hyperbole, the tautology.

Conspirare is being shepherded, assemblage of human sounds.

VII.

Fr Gabriel leans again, head against armored breast,
St Gabriel the Archangel
                swathing white raiment, mantle of light.

Is this what Daniel, Zechariah, Mother Mary saw?

I asked once the nature of true ethereal light:

> *What is the white light*
> > *of God's love,*
> *its clear form and nature and property*

> > > *and definition?*

VIII.

Good words have become alluring again
—this, the language that speaks
> of worth and love and virtue.

> *Yes, love, again and again, yet again.*

> *Only a holy love, that I ask for always,*
> > *yes, yes, yes*

> > > *to the eternal yes.*

Today's homily tells me to suspend judgment
—no gazing at the splinter, spindle in anyone's eye
without pulling out the plank in mine,
> pried from the years
> of so many words,
> so many futile, fruitless words.

So, no words today, love tells me as warrant and counsel.

So, here's the music, in all its wordless, ineffable glory—
> caught in midair,
> carefully attended and listened to.

This exact moment, of morning breaking, crisp cusp of dawn.

This must be an exercise, along with response song and daylight.

This must be a spiritual exercise, its own temperance,
> I tell myself now.

Small Acts of Translation

What shifts, what loss of meaning?

What can one language hold
that another simply can't, doesn't know what to do with?

Contraction—*that happens*—that manner of drainage.

Attenuation, like a weakening of personal will.

No forceps to pick up a clause, pry it apart, skeletal.
No forcefulness,
as if the empty caesurae issued their own certain movement.

Like destiny, if you believe in it.

That definitive definition of what's to come, how things will end.

Lee Hi trills the high notes of "Breathe".
In translation, what's happening is a desperate love—
one conscientious other, trying to help the other breathe.

There's an uplift, updraft scaling new heights,
each elevation
one more step toward reprieve, a measured bliss.

The singer breathes, each enunciation as exasperated.

The other day, Judith Beveridge spoke
of poetry
as linguistic art, a formulation around breathing,

and not.

Translation Memory,
and Your Principle of Reduction?

"True translation is transparent: it does not obscure
the original, does not stand in its light, but rather allows
pure language, as if strengthened by its own medium,
to shine even more fully on the original."

Walter Benjamin

Do you see the rising of air, not wisps, in a swirl?

Do you see my new life after non-breath?

How could you—you weren't there, you were never there.

That wasn't a question, I was not asking.
That last statement was as definite a stoppage as the question.

The non-question, like the fourteen lines of a nonce sonnet.

Death, its breathlessness, presents itself as negative space.

Sudden undoing of a life of everything,
that's the crude expunging.

Do you see the chemistry now,
                    the oxidation-reduction, how it changes things?

The rusting faucet, even as water still drips from it.

The halved apple and potato, left to their own browning—
                    how open-faced their bareness,
                    look at how defeated each surface looks.

Do you see the wildfire, its blaze so incandescent,
                    it ignites and animates the night sky?

There,
    houses and plains burning away,
        down to ash and dead earth.

There goes someone's dossier of lived life,
    and every effort to archive
    what was precious and important.

You ask yourself years after: *what matter?*

            What mattered, after all?
            What matters, as an insistence?

Call it a countermand, an existential reversal of fortune.

Unless.

Unless, the rescission is but a dismantling
    of what didn't work, the awfulness
    and all that bad.

Unless from what's scrubbed out
comes a clean slate—
    spotless,
    saved floor and form.

After Chiaroscuro

"That poetry survived in its formal agencies finally,
and that prose survived to get something said."

Robert Creeley

This is about settling on an image.

Imagine the Imagists in the room, filled with their banter.

Every confession is an exposition, centered on a single thing.

Not what the thing is, but what it looks like, seems like.

The drama of tenebrism, that sharpness
                of contrast and counterpoint,
                  to make clearer such distinctions
                    —what's sunlit,
                            backlit,
                  the hiddenness of shadow.

What visual metaphor it can become.

        That sort of power, says Robert Creeley.
        And absence of power, says Lorine Niedecker.

        What is power, after all,
                after all
            is said and done?

A flash of staged light;
a kind of burnt-out, burnished complexion,
                    in retrospect.

A simple figment, not one even of the imagination.

An empty but love-filled spotlight,
                thinning varnish on hardwood floor.

Tenebrism Again, In Relief

"Love is not consolation. It is light."
Simone Weil

In Caravaggio's own words: *Amor Vincit Omnia.*

It must have been an ode to Virgil's Eclogue X,
how Virgil has returned to his home village, Andes.

Look at the different cut and strain of logic here.

Fact is: the unilinear is an unreasonable expectation of art.

Virgil was his own guide,
the long trek from Milan up north to the flatland of Mantua.

The Latin in translation: *[That] Love conquers all.*

The love has remained capitalized,
an effect I find something of an earned appearance
and purchase for my poetry these days.

Did I actually just confess
that remote intentionality, that aesthetic
              denial-and-removal-turned-allowance?

Look at Caravaggio's *Deposition of Christ.*
It hangs, like history, in the Vatican Pinacoteca.

              Christ's body,
              luminous skin defying every working
                    of light, its effortless rise and fall
                    like nature,
                    its owned and abstract rhythms,
              the way light travels in logical directions.

[I never minded the monologic, if it brought me Truth.]

The fourth wall breaks,
entire scene—descent from the Cross—foregrounded.

Foreshortened tomb ledge, and bent elbow.

These Baroque artists knew how to collapse
the inside-outside within canvas
        with the real outside—of our evolving world.

We watch tradition, animated through light and dark.

Willing or not, we are involved
                vis-à-vis our closed-in gaze.

What character do we allow ourselves to become thus?

What narrator, what person beyond the mouthed,
                the made known?

Mere accessory-in-waiting, ready to help.

                God forbid, an antagonist.

        Maybe adherent and aide;
        spreader of the faith
                like in the good old days.

        What beloved, given apostolate then?

        What lyric calling for today?

The Act of Movement

"Beauty is the disinterested one, without which
the ancient world refused to understand itself,
a word which both imperceptibly and yet unmistakably
has bid farewell to our new world, a world of interests,
leaving it to its own avarice and sadness."

Hans Urs von Balthasar

Art isn't therapy, that's the new jingle.

Art isn't bloodletting, no go-to place for treatment.

Art shouldn't carry that burdened agency.

Art, beyond all assumptions, should be free.

Art, never the recuperative or reformative.

Art isn't court of any sort, no restitution of lost things.

Even ruin of the Good, the need to restore such cost, such wrong.

Art can reauthor abuse, wound, distress, any affliction.

Yet, *Art*—remains too damaged itself, to wake from its induced sleep.

Art writhes; and racked, can only convulse.

Art as pencil shavings, snatch and lick of light.

Art sampling, each grain, each flake, each slice, each sliver.

Art as manifest fractured emotion, as Beauty would say.

Art as Beauty, which Diotima spoke of in *The Symposium*.

Art as Beauty as Love, as Socrates withdraws into the dialogic.

Art, as eidetic—*memory of a memory*—if it remembers at all.

Art, indeed, is its own long-suffering inner condition.

Art, strange victim of its own declaimed terms of condition.

Art remains an indictment of its subject/object of affection.

Art—*but what of Virtue?* The love that wills the good of others.

Art as death to its subject, dream and slumber, trance-like.

Art as dying to itself; no trance, no, but peaceful.

Art as becalmed state, today's rest of respite.

Art, stilled into eternal meaning—eternal, repose.

Fides Quaerens Intellectum

"It is very much our mission to transform the
prose of this life into poetry, into heroic verse."

Saint Josemaría Escrivá, *Furrow*

I.

I picked up a cube of rock, dislodged.
It stood on its own, at an angle against the evening light.
It cast a shadow perhaps, so slight a shade of gray.

Unmottled like its skin,
surface like a thick rind sealed in.

Because rock *is* rock, no unpeeling of things and circumstance.

Theology isn't something loft-high or faraway

—*ungettable.*

Theology begets itself, in its own making and unmasking.

"Theology is just faith seeking understanding."

My divinity professor said it,
just as St Augustine said it.

Carved-out.

Clutch and clasp.

Of sudden snatched-up phrase.

I know that now, *fides quaerens intellectum*, the way of thought.

And plumbed depth of every feeling,
by way of only the Holy Spirit.

This and that,
the way of reimagination of the old days, old ways.

This and that,
St Anselm of Canterbury unworried in exile, as faraway.
As out of reach, like the logic of yesterday.

As remote, the problem of evil something no one wants to contemplate.

As undone, the agency of the Pontius Pilates of the day.

As monstrous the betrayal foretold;
but how it was a pivot.

To lead to the Cross.

That salvific moment, of history entire.

II.

That priest's reminder—*old sins cast long shadows*,
as idiom would have it.

*That the longest way round is the shortest way home,
our enviable long way home.*

One idiom, followed by another.

In contradistinction.

This and that—*credo ut intelligam*, as St Anselm of Canterbury said it.

"I believe so that I may understand," I know that now.

Today, then tomorrow.

Today and tomorrow.

Forevermore,
to the end of my ingathered, long-form days.

Triptych:
Iteration of Only Importance

"Thou art worthy, O Lord, to receive glory
and honour and power: for thou hast created all things,
and for thy pleasure they are and were created."

Revelation 4:11

Reginald Heber hummed his new words. To what tune, he might have wondered? Just as we might wonder, before *Nicaea* took hold, gave language-form another incline and flection of form? John Bacchus Dykes must have read in the words what he read in the music, as if the music came from somewhere else other than himself. Paul Croft's piano is simple, every note and musical phrase plainly played, open-and-shut, like the Holy Bible over morning hour. That motion, too, like this hymn, take me to church.

Finally, I get to use words like *glory* and *majesty* and *holy* and *praise*, and allow them to mean what they mean—within my lyric, completely comprehensible.

Unadorned, unburnished.

What is it like to stand in your father's own parish, and look down on the pews you rested in as a child? What is the expressed church— *and churching*, your grandmother asks you—that you remember? The churching must have been both intimate and shared, your grandmother reminds you, a memory of her so long ago, your mind can barely offer a picture. An imago, for Lacan, is the ideal mother perhaps? The face of devotion, now a portrait within the mirror. A stage and station, and as grandmother hopes too, a state of grace.

Mother Mary, as grandmother would have liked to say, as the family moves through each week of Advent. The imago as imagined, beyond the Latin notion of "image", beyond the entomological insistence of a definition. Of the winged aphid, in its crowning stage, after its endmost ecdysis, that shedding of last skin. The masks come off, along with the veils and shawls and one's whole raiment of threads and trappings.

Nonesuch, as it were, because only an old word could stay close enough to such intended effect.

What is imago beyond ideation, beyond its own shape and appearance?

Of the reimagined imago?

The mother yellowjacket, overwintering—overwintered, with what tired, luminous face will it emerge, show its small, provisional world?

Holy, Holy, Holy. As now sung by Audrey Assad, her voice in a soft trill in the high notes, risen to the rafters. In the middle register, there is steady comfort. *Blessed Assurance*, as it were, as written by Fanny Crosby.

Crosby was blind, her thin-rimmed glasses like onyx cabochons. Not vacant sockets, nothing frightening like that, of life emptied out. You know obsidian is black—how it names itself, christened for its unmistakable character—but who knew one could find black opal and black spinel? Schorl tourmaline is black night too, its striations barely there. So is your Tahitian pearl, which you will never sell, you say. It is the reminder of kingdom—in the here and now, what's happily to come—that great price and, indeed, treasure.

The first line of the hymn was Crosby's sententious answer to her friend Phoebe Knapp's question: "What do you think the tune says?" The tune, also simply made—in the sitting room, on a castaway piano—came before the words.

What was India like on 3 April, 1826? You ask this, as if anyone could know of things that happened so long ago. Heber died that day, you say, somewhere in Tiruchirappalli, Madras. He was 42, the age of your father when he finally walked in his own shoes. When your father understood parental duty for what it was, less obligation than a real fealty. Not to child, no, not that; rather, a promise to God. Heber was already Bishop of Calcutta. Dykes was a man of the cloth too. He made it to vicar of St Oswald's, a parish church in Durham.

Dykes is still writing song, knowing the gift of music, beyond the gift of words. Heber is still writing lyric, knowing the gift of words formally chosen and invoked, then strung along, one phrasal turn after a verisimilar other.

Beyond their own natural, effortless, internal

heard song.

Holy Holy Holy   Holy Holy Holy   Holy Holy Holy
Holy Holy Holy   Holy Holy Holy   Holy Holy Holy
Holy Holy Holy   Holy Holy Holy   Holy Holy Holy
Holy Holy Holy   Holy Holy Holy   Holy Holy Holy
Holy Holy Holy   Holy Holy Holy   Holy Holy Holy
Holy Holy Holy   Holy Holy Holy   Holy Holy Holy
Holy Holy Holy   Holy Holy Holy   Holy Holy Holy
Holy Holy Holy   Holy Holy Holy   Holy Holy Holy
Holy Holy Holy   Holy Holy Holy   Holy Holy Holy
Holy Holy Holy   Holy Holy Holy   Holy Holy Holy
Holy Holy Holy   Holy Holy Holy   Holy Holy Holy
Holy Holy Holy   Holy Holy Holy   Holy Holy Holy
Holy Holy Holy   Holy Holy Holy   Holy Holy Holy
Holy Holy Holy   Holy Holy Holy   Holy Holy Holy

Postmeridian Dalí

After Crucifixion (Corpus Hypercubus), 1954

"No one can become and remain a theologian unless
he is compelled again and again to be astonished at himself."

Karl Barth

there are only
so many hours a day

i'm starting
to forget

days can be unhurried
and slow-moving

measured
in the meter of minutiae

puncture the three quarters
like wounds

two clean slits
on upfaced palms

no gore or gushing blood
no such stirring

of history's great tragedy
singular

sacrifice
mirror of one afternoon

mirrored across time
and every space

conceivable
yours and mine in turn

at once
one with the world

Postmeridian Dalí II

After The Ascension of Christ, 1958

"God has not the slightest need for our proofs."

Karl Barth

this afternoon walk
of science

i'm starting
to remember

cosmic dreams
make for their truth

someone is in step
ahead

blind to conversation
wind-thrown

each statement
another position

mislaid
slow-going ricochet

like flat stone
readied

agreed, let us
note the difference:

stone skipping
or stone skimming

how many times
to bounce the idea

how far to go
before finality

Ordinary Time

"Like a rising star (cf. Num 24:17), Jesus comes to enlighten all peoples
and to brighten the nights of humanity. Today, with the Magi, let us lift our
eyes to heaven and ask: 'Where is the child who has been born?' (Mt 2:2).
Where can we find and encounter our Lord?"

Pope Francis

There are limits, a place
                of dead ends,
to the rhizome.

It doesn't sprawl,
                after all,
        the way you used to think.

The way you used to think—

                what does this smallness,
                this small epiphany mean?

What do all of life's small moments mean?

+

The rhizome does not posit
                an adequate answer
to these things of the day.

The rhizome is but a symptom
                of these things.

I return to the tree,
        after all the years—
        where I first began.

        To think of things,
                        these things
        of comings and goings.

+

It's Ordinary Time again.

Ordinary Time,
when we wear green again.

I think of this
as celebrating Saint Patrick's Day
every day—

the prayer
that Christ is everywhere.

+

"There's an excellent clip by Bishop Barron on faith and reason."
"Peter Kreeft has great ones on philosophy, theology, even Tolkien."
"It's Christmas, catch Bishop's sermon on God becoming a baby."
"Did you watch *The Chosen* episode that's just gone viral?"
"Yup, the Samaritan woman at the well. Wept like a baby."
"Jesus walks on water. They pulled out all the stops for that episode."
"Simon fiercely clinging to Jesus in the storm? Boy did I ugly-cry."
"Yup, they bring out the best moments in these gospel stories."
"Yup, Jonathan Roumie really brings out the humanity in Jesus."
"What about that film where Shia LaBeouf plays Padre Pio?"
"The stigmatic! Padre Pio is amazing, just like St Francis of Assisi."
"St Catherine of Siena. St Gemma Galgani. St Rita of Cascia also."
"Yup. For his prep, LaBeouf spent time at a Capuchin monastery."
"You should catch *Cabrini*. Cristiana Dell'Anna aces the role."
"St Frances Xavier Cabrini rocks—seriously, that nun's ambition!"
"Yup. Cabrini became our first American saint. Canonized 1946."
"Nice. Go check out Fr Andrew Dalton on *Pints With Aquinas*."
"Mind-blowing stuff—the scholarship on the Shroud of Turin."
"Awesome. Fr Mike Schmitz's apostolate is phenomenal, I think."
"Everyone loves his voice and energy. And he just says it like it is."
"He's on *Ascension Presents*. Fr Mark-Mary, Sr Mary Grace too."
"Christ is everywhere, like you said. Like St Patrick's prayer says."
"Bishop has a great clip on the qualities of the Good Shepherd."
"I have a Good Shepherd statuette. From Traditions Monastiques."
"Ah, the abbey of St Joseph Clairval in France. Did they bless it?"
"Yup, the monks are the best. *Good Shepherd Carrying a Lamb*."
"Fourth century, correct? Domitilla Catacombs, Vatican Museums."
"Yup. Might get the St Wendelin of Trier statue too, from Italy."
"If you're looking for patrons of shepherds, there's St Bernadette."

"Of Lourdes—nice! St Drogo and St Regina. St Germaine Cousin."
"Wow, LaBeouf is now a Catholic. Bishop Barron confirmed him."
"Whoa, so is Tammy Peterson, the wife of Jordan Peterson."
"Have you read *Rome Sweet Home* by the Hahns? Phenomenal."
"Tammy's story about her miraculous healing did go crazy viral too."
"Yup, her cancer just went away, thanks to her praying the rosary."
"By God's grace, her prayer intentions and petitions were heard."
"The Lord willing, her testimony will open more hearts and minds."
"Love how the clip ends—she prays the Our Father and Hail Mary."

+

        Ordinary Time—
and looking for the extraordinary
            within.

     Now that yesterday is *yesterday*.
     Now, with the Feast of Epiphany ended, celebrated.
     Now, how the wise men looked to the Light of the Star.

How, Saint Thomas Aquinas knew the meaning of signs.

     How they worked.

     What language
           and geography
       they spoke.

     How, now

     —notice this,
     know this—
     the wise men
     worshipped

     the Infant
     Jesus

     without
     a ready home

        or
        welcome.

Overheard at Walled Churchyard

"It is in the midst of the most material things of the earth
that we must sanctify ourselves, serving God and all mankind."

Saint Josemaría Escrivá

"They finally made the film on St Andrew Kim."
"Stay with me, Lord, in my stillness; show me Your will."
"Mother Mary's fiat. Learn from that."
"A lesson in every single thing, don't we realize by now?"
"—darker the days, more difficult the discernment."
"Taegon, you forgot Taegon. Too many Kims in Korea."
"He's a Saint. How far wrong can you go, looking for him?"
"*Let it be done.* Now that's what I call obedience."
"Not to self, in these unreal times. Me Generation, and all."
"You mean Me Me Me Generation, that's where we're at."
"That's where the world is at—"
"I don't recognize the world anymore; do you?"
"It does get tough."
"Am I in it?"
"You don't count. You're not on social media."
"I don't?"
"You don't."
"Oh."
"Yup."
"Yup."
"Et Cetera—"
"Et Cetera."
"Read Hegel. He has a theory of recognition."
"Works for intersubjectivity, which you like to talk about."
"What do we have in common?"
"What is shared between both of us, just us?"
"What is perceived in this sharing, you mean?"
"I guess—I wanted to say *whatever*, but…"
"That would have been impolite."
"—but not disingenuous."
"Indeed, the way this world seems these days."
"Dark days."

"Dark, postmodern days."

"Indeed."

"Recognition."

"It's happening right now. Recognition theory."

"Yes."

"Yes, we do agree on some things."

"The world—that too."

"What about that? What about the world?"

"The world is happening right now, that too."

"Oh."

"Don't recognize it—"

"Really?"

"We don't recognize it."

"That changed everything."

"What did?"

"The inclusion of one word—*we*."

"I can see the italics of your speech act."

"Nice."

"Nice."

"Korea has a long list of Saints."

"Yes, the Korean Martyrs."

"I think I might buy that statue of St Kim."

"You have a whole bunch of statues already."

"Yup."

"Yup."

"I'm drawn to the beauty."

"In concert with the True and the Good."

"The only way Beauty should speak."

"The only kind I recognize these days."

"I might go for the St Kateri Tekakwitha too."

"Go for it."

"You think? What about Bl Carlo Acutis?"

"Very soon the world's first millennial saint."

"Yup."

"Go for it, yup."

"You approve, for real?"

"Sanctify the ordinary, right?"

"Yup."

"Yup—et cetera."

"Et cetera."

"Let it be done."

Villanelle of Fairly Recent Memes-Turned-Screenshots on My iPhone Conscientiously Typed Out Because of the Work Asked of The Work

1. Psalms 33:9—
    For he spoke, and it came to be, commanded,
    and it stood in place.

2. Isaiah 14:27—
    For the Lord Almighty has purposed,
    and who can thwart him?
    His hand is stretched out,
    and who can turn it back?

3. Joshua 1:9—
    Have I not commanded you?
    Be strong and courageous. Do not be afraid;
    do not be discouraged, for the Lord your God
    will be with you wherever you go.

4. Sirach 35:2—
    Returning a kindness is like a grain offering;
    giving to the poor
    is like a thanksgiving offering.

5. Mark 11:25—
    And when you stand and pray, forgive anything
    you may have against anyone,
    so that your Father in heaven
    will forgive the wrongs you have done.

6. Psalms 41:13—
    Everyone praise the Lord God of Israel,
    always and forever! For he is from eternity past
    and will remain for the eternity to come.
    That's the way it will be forever.
    Faithful is our King! Amen.

7. Ephesians 3:19–20—
    And may you know his love, even though
    it can't be known completely.
    Then you will be filled with everything
    God has for you. God is able to do far
    more than we could ever ask for or
    imagine. He does everything by
    his power that is working in us.

8. John 17:24—
    Father! You have given them to me,
    and I want them to be with me where I am,
    so that they may see my glory,
    the glory you gave me;
    for you loved me before the world was made.

9. Romans 8:38–39— For I am convinced that neither death nor life,
neither angels nor demons,
neither the present nor the future,
nor any powers, neither height nor depth,
nor anything else in all creation,
will be able to separate us from
the love of God that is in
Christ Jesus our Lord.

10. Psalms 147:3— He heals the brokenhearted and binds up their wounds.
11. Psalms 68:6— He gives the lonely a home to live in
and leads prisoners out
into happy freedom,
but rebels will have to live
in a desolate land.
12. Psalms 121:5— The Lord himself watches over you!
The Lord stands beside you
as your protective shade.

13. John 19:27— Behold, your Mother!
14. John 16:24— Until now you have not asked for anything
in my name; ask and you will receive,
so that your happiness may be complete.
15. Psalms 32:8— I will guide you along the best pathway
for your life.
I will advise you
and watch over you.

16. Acts 1:14— All these were continually devoting themselves
with one mind to prayer,
along with the women,
and Mary the mother of Jesus,
and with His brothers.
17. Mark 12:30— Love the Lord your God with all your heart
and with all your soul
and with all your mind
and with all your strength.
18. John 17:17— Consecrate them in the truth. Your word is truth.
19. Revelation 21:3–4— Behold, the dwelling of God is with men.
He will dwell with them, and they shall be
his people, and God himself will be with them;
he will wipe away every tear from their eyes,
and death shall be no more,
neither shall there be mourning
nor crying nor pain any more,
for the former things have passed away.

How Did Fish Become This Hour, This Narrative Memory?

> "He performs wonders that cannot be fathomed,
> miracles that cannot be counted."
>
> Job 5:9

I.

My priest likes the first miracle within the Johannine Gospel. He says his country's wine is good enough. If you want wine, please choose a good wine. Port wine from the Douro Valley. That's good enough.

Memory only allows itself to be accessed, with the admission. The personal yes to a yes, but not in the way you understood it those years ago, when you thought you understood these things.

To understand these things, this would be the kind of elevated diction frowned upon nowadays.

Today, there's no face of disapproval, none of the affectation of false fronts the world has grown into.

What is it like to read the land?

II.

"Unless you people see signs and wonders," Jesus told him, *"you will never believe."*

John 4:48. You lift it from the epigraph, that original placement now looking at once coincident and attendant, the added speech marks suddenly evincing. If Jesus said it—if those are actually what Jesus said, highlighted in red in your Bible. If the gospel writers allowed the memory to state itself. If the years in between didn't mist or make indistinct the moment, the good of the moment.

This early morning, the litany of ifs no longer hover in the old indecision, that undecidability you used to love.

So, the speech marks don't need to be there.

You don't need the hint of history promised in an epigraph.

You don't need that reification, if the object of history has become real.

Even if merely in the language, that symbolic world, that universe of relational meaning.

Even in the painstaking, faultless detailing. Even good intent can miss the mark. Beauty, it seems, takes one more step, blithely inch-perfect. Fat dumb and happy, but always in the direction of truth, we agree. Not crudely or rudely so—but the bald bluntness does say it like it is, we also agree.

III.

Over a year after, you look up *real presence*, the church documents making for clarity and the obedience you already accept as part and parcel of these important things. Of identity and proper formation, a steadying humility that begins again and again. And again, *nunc coepi*, which translates from Latin to mean: "Now I begin."

That clause doesn't need a full stop to punctuate the pause, or any end-stopped line in a lyric contemplation, this afternoon moment suddenly quiet. This afternoon moment has become its own breezeless, breathless pastoral.

IV.

What would Saussure have thought of what Pope Paul VI penned in the 1965 encyclical *Mysterium fidei*? What can theory do if all it does is unfasten and separate?

There is truth in this, you say. There is truth in transubstantiation.

Strangely, the games of language-making don't necessarily rise to the occasion.

To encounter truth as it is—to say it properly and reverently, as these things should be said.

To witness a Eucharistic miracle, its acknowledgment through the sheer numbers, the numberless adherents over land and sea, and land and sea again.

To live so close to nature, ear to earth, to the tremor of ground and the times. To see the lope of white-tailed deer so far away, across the ridge, as if from another country. This knowledge is an intuition and a definitive logic, another kind of familiar territory. Familiarity is a kind of recognition, of something old, now an echo, a mirror, a new wrinkle on your brow, the face that looks back at you from the pool.

V.

The familiarity of memory, how it has turned into narrative memory in a moment, how peculiar and particular the experience of the moment.

But how beautiful the language can make of its own old, distant thought.

Not far-flung—just so long ago, you can't even remember the decade.

VI.

I have the *St Joseph Pocket Prayer Book* in my left pants pocket. I take it with me everywhere I go. It starts with an explanation of the Mass, subtitling it "Essence of the Mass".

People don't know what to do with truth these days, nevermind the recognition of it.

People like to think they walk on the safe side, keep far left on the shoulder and sidewalk. Left shoulder chafing against craggy wall. They speak of notions and the temporal and the perceived. Of phenomenology. But they don't know what to do with something as absolute as truth.

I still have four copies of *Seven Joys & Sorrows of St Joseph*. It is edited by Father Jose Luis Lopez Carpio. It is a beautifully made book, white as snow. There is an inscription in it by Father Joe.

Within my pocket prayer book is the Litany of St Joseph. Before it is the Litany of the Blessed Virgin Mary. After it is the Litany of the Sacred Heart of Jesus. It's wonderful how calming the recitative can become, the cycle of rhythm and petition like good, kingly song.

Within my pocket prayer book are also several prayers of the Saints. St Patrick's prayer was just mentioned in today's homily, which arrives each morning through my phone. The intercessory prayers to St Peregrine and St Pio of Pietrelcina seem especially poignant for these pandemic days too.

Some kid told Father Joe the Mass was so boring, Father Joe mentioned in one homily. He told the kid: *You are boring. You bring nothing to the Mass.*

You can bring your intentions, Father Joe said.

There is so much to pray for these days.

There is so much work to be done in these strange and bizarre, truth-defying days.

VII.

What is it like to have worry, already a grief, over that Capernaum boy? What is it like to travel far to beg for a miracle?

What is it like to be a father? To have a son at all, and that sudden moment in his life made purpose, when doubt is turned into belief?

A willing suspension of disbelief, this is not the appropriate phrase to put to use here, we agree.

For whom again is the pond not a mirror today—or ever, has it ever been? They ask with genuine interest, strangely never of themselves to find the experience and answer. The pond of their knowing is not a still surface, to depict a symmetry of likeness, truth reflection, despite its own oblique portraiture. A mirage, no less. A refraction—its subtle, gentle parsing.

The pond of such knowing is not the same miracle.

VIII.

Look for the miracle. Look for the sign and wonder, the greatest prayer there is.

IX.

Look for the miracle, and accept the miracle. Believe the miracle.

You understand this now.

X.

My priest likes to cite the first miracle, when so much of it was already telling and a gifting of eternal gifts.

The turning of water into wine. The wedding at Cana. John 4:48. The same Cana, where the signs and wonders began. Why the return to an origin, the place of starting points?

That early source is a fount, its water pooled, this baptismal font.

Why do we return to first places? Why do we return to old memory?

Again and again. And again *again.*

Why do we look at first love, and say:

> you're worth the wait—
> you're worth my lifetime of longing.

Sonnet to Adoration
of the Holy Eucharist: List Poem

"Very truly, I tell you, whoever believes has eternal life.
I am the bread of life. Your ancestors ate the manna in the wilderness,
and they died. This is the bread that comes down from heaven,
so that one may eat of it and not die. I am the living bread that came
down from heaven. Whoever eats of this bread will live forever;
and the bread that I will give for the life of the world is my flesh."

John 6:47–51

I.   As Jesus said, *For my flesh is true food and my blood is true drink*

II.   Saint Paul's reminder and exhortation in I Corinthians II:17–34

III.   Saint Comgall's chrismal to the rescue—Lord as refuge and Redeemer

IV.   Pope Gregory VII against Berengarius' error, signed profession of faith

V.   Pope Urban IV and the Feast of Corpus Christi, Christ with us all days

VI.   Saint Thomas Aquinas, his three hymns after the Miracle of Bolsena

VII.   Pope Martin V against the Calixtines on species, entire Body and Blood

VIII.   Pope Clement VIII, his *Quarantore*, our forty hours of pure devotion

IX.   Saint Peter Julian Eymard's cause, Perpetual Adoration among us laity

X.   Pope John Paul II, the duty of Eucharistic Congresses since 1881

XI.   Pope Leo XIII, Nocturnal Adoration, his joy and the bearing of fruit

XII.   Pope Pius X, the bounty of nourishment for the Church's intimate life

XIII.   Blessed Virgin Mary, our devotion at Benediction of the Blessed Sacrament

XIV.   So help us, God, may we always adore, entreat the Real Presence of Christ

Flipped Classroom Catechism

"Jesus answered them and said,
'My doctrine is not Mine, but His who sent Me.'"

John 7:16

The Bishop Barron clip is good
—*just send it, and see what happens.*

Let it speak for itself.
Let the Holy Spirit move them.

The other day spoke of salvation,
which souls would be saved.

That titling should have scared
the hell out of everyone.

Careful here not to be using
scare the bejesus out of someone...

What about
scaring the bejeebers out of anyone?

[...   ...   .   ]
[...   ...   .   ]

Once, someone said he'd confess
for her, no?—neither knew any better.

It must be hard to do penance
for that someone else, you tell yourself.

[...   ...   .   ]
[...   ...   .   ]

What did Jesus say from the Cross?
The seven last words—the first saying?

Father, forgive them;
for they do not know what they are doing.

There, as Luke 23:34 goes, before
Jesus commends His spirit to the Father.

[...   ...   .   ]
[...   ...   .   ]

If we confess our sins,
He is faithful

and just to forgive us our sins, and
to cleanse us from all unrighteousness.

That there was 1 John 1:9.
This here is Matthew 6:15—

But if you do not forgive others their sins,
your Father will not forgive your sins.

[...   ...   .   ]
[...   ...   .   ]

But is that wokeism enough?
But it's not for one to expect forgiveness.

Say sorry, that's the dictum,
but forgiveness is theirs to give.

Not ours, or yours, to assume?
Not ours or anyone's—to count on?

[...   ...   .   ]
[...   ...   .   ]

What would St Augustine say to this?
What was today's quote of the day?

"If you are suffering from a bad man's
injustice, forgive him—lest there be

two bad men."
Do we hear his urging, clear bidding?

Indeed, do we heed the Saints' caution,
inspired counsel roused by Scripture?

[... ... ...]
[... ... ...]

Another blended moment
one sent text, leaning to the next.

[... ... ...]
[... ... ...]

What was St Peter thinking then?
What was the moment like, the trigger

—of memory, or feeling?
Maybe just the hint of a sound.

Whiff and trace of a forgotten scent.
Sight, what does it mean to see in these days?

[... ... ...]
[... ... ...]

Then Peter came to Him and said,
"Lord, how often shall my brother sin against me,

and I forgive him? Until seven times?"
And Jesus said unto him,

"I say not unto thee, until seven times,
but until seventy times seven."

That there was Matthew 18:21–22.
Sent, resent. Then *sent*. Sent—

Unshod, Thoughts of Unselfing

"The soul that journeys to God, but doesn't shake off its cares
and quiet its appetites, is like someone who drags a cart of dirt uphill."

Saint John of the Cross

Saint John of the Cross is seated alone,
shadow on three walls.

This cell,
one-man,
but a hole in a wall.

Did you know Hole-in-the-Wall is an actual place?

South Africa's Eastern Cape,
this archway of rock, stone and shale.

The Xhosa people have
their name for it too—Place of the Sound.

Or, is it Place of Noise?

How the earth has known itself
for over two hundred million years.

+

This isn't about this or that
shame
about what it means to write
what it means
to be a writer, at all.

What is sound,
all over again?

What, who sounds the noise?

After all, the writing of worth—
what did Father say
about the teleological again?

+

The Discalced Carmelites have come and gone.

They left behind
their Saint Teresa of Avila statue
for you,
for us—

on purpose, I think.

+

I write, and worth becomes a question
of being,
of design, not
from the derivations
from within, but
of purpose
and destination.

+

You're still writing the writing
that wounds,
did you know?

+

Did you know that for yourself
when language was its own impulse,
and narrative became
a being,
both terminus and intention

—what manner of
resting place

                ad interim?

+

Do you know that now,
        all along the line?

Do you know of these things now
        of being
        all the same—

        and what it means
        to walk discalceate

                within
        this endemic imprint

                all the hours
                God sends?

Episodic Memory,
What Memorabilia-Made-Explicit

1.1

This is a list poem, or at least desires to begin as one.
                                        An inception, like a small gifting.

Of a blessed waking up into conscious things,
what needs to be said this early morning.

I think of first thoughts
and odes and living saints
and the day I decided to be a pilgrim
(although no one really decides these important things).

2.4

That wandering into Malacca. Over a decade ago. Sarong for a bag, big knot over my shoulder. I only ever wore black—crew neck tee and fisherman pants—to be non-descript, and disappear like every other dull, humdrum thing.

2.7

The look of poverty gets you spat upon (but divinity school made me brood, think up ways of ascetic living). A group of students talked about beating me up. An old man at a kopitiam told me I wasn't welcome. *We're a small town,* he said, *we don't want trouble.*

The town here isn't the town there. There are so many towns, all of them different in peculiar ways. You can't tell a town from a day's stay, or even after a month or year.

4.1

Self-denial, like this Lenten season of greater intention.
More fasting, more prayer, more alms-giving.

There's a rush to the couplet, like something of the hastened heroic
—no need for delineation and breakage; what defined lines and stanzas?

3.5

Who is he, where is he from? Will we find him dead in the morning?
Check his bag. Check his hotel room upon check-out.

(Did I look that desolate, was everything so morose,
                            as much as everyone in the small town
                            depicted things to be?)

How did he die the first time? Did he kill himself in the attic?

(Does the memory look that dismal, so tragic?)

39.40

There is the ideal reader.
There is the inscribed or implied reader, how implicit meaning becomes.
There is the thoughtful reader, who reads the way writers read and write.

There is the empirical reader,
                        and everyone else's tall walls,
                        all their unvoiced limits of interpretation.

                        What of *intentio operis*?

                        ....

                        ....

                        ....

                        What of *intentio lectoris*?

8.2

In South Bend, Indiana, a kind man walked up to me at the grotto, and
told me life wasn't that bad. That must have been 2008 or 2009, when I
wanted to visit the lake, but steer clear of deep water. I wished he'd given
me a religious tract, something to keep in my wallet, some pamphlet on

grief and salvation.

(Now, I collect holy cards, and give them to anyone who wants them.)

Stay close to piety, I told myself, *hang on to any handrail.*

Sacred, grace-filled places and things.

Offer up your suffering to God with complete love and abandon.
Offer up your suffering to God for the salvation of souls,
                                        especially your own.

In some cities, they call you a dog, talk about stripping you bare, leave
you naked—so you'll beg like a dog for your clothes back. Here, they
make plans to steal your money after, say the world would be better off
without people like that.

There's a casualness to confession, you've been taught
                            —crispness, the starkness
                of one's own cognition and acceptance.

3.7

....

....

....

(Do these look like coded ciphers, or erasure,
a kind of white-out redaction vis-à-vis double-barrelled ellipses?)

(What of paratext as threshold? Of meaning, what is read—
                            which peritexts emerge, maintain?
                Which epitexts find their way,
                situate themselves, resonate and fill the air?
What of hypotext and hypertext,
the myriad hypertexts and how they travel?
                What of the hypertext that begins again,
                            becomes its own hypotext?
                What was aforesaid and foregoing?
What seemed and became subsequent, even consequential?)

2.9

The pink rosary someone left behind on a pew.

They didn't forget to take it. It's left behind on purpose, as a blessing.

It's left behind for someone else.

(Which town is this now?
This town isn't the same town, or is it?

        Who can read the signs,
     especially the ones that point to somewhere beyond a hill?
     And you already know there are so many towns.
     Where has the bus-to-nowhere taken me cross-state?)

5.8

Christ Church Malacca is pink too, like a robust coral or roseate. The Dutch started building it in 1741, took twelve years before it was finished. It was actually all white, until 1911. By then, it was an Anglican church.

Facades change, even whole identities and constitutions.

Some historical things don't change though, like Christ Church, and how it's still the oldest working Protestant church in the country.

It's nice to have warm pews. Wood doesn't turn cold, like leatherette or wrought iron.

It's nice to have churches filled with people and song.

7.4

....

....

....

This is a series of elliptical phrases, saying things halfway.

(Is the adjective elliptical here used to connote
a shaping of thought and feeling as curvature?
      Or is it talking of a concision through omission?
      Or as a counterpoint,
      like a protracted dramatic monologue
      rambling in a periphrastic sprawl, into tedium?)

11.9

I still have memorabilia from that trip
      —pink rosary in a coin purse,
    made of barn straw, its big and bold stripes
    of pink, green and white, like a Newfoundland flag.

11.12

This is a list poem, I remember.
      Its tricolor re-authoring
      and recollection.

I'd like to visit this large island,
as if to step into a world hitherto unknown, untouched.

I'd like to visit St Pius X Church, the modesty of its red brick.
Look at its vast parking lot, ideal for our open-air soup kitchen.

I'd like to go to Montreal too,
      visit the Archive of the Jesuits in Canada.

How small and distant, how alien and quaint we must seem here.

11.38

The provincial capital is St John's, that's what they named it.

That's what they decided on;
every act of naming is a conscientious, conscious choice,
      we'd like to think,
      a decision-in-the-making.

    As deliberate as studied, thoughtful care.

As deliberate as tomorrow's confession.

People in love with language
inevitably like the sound of names,
          and the reason for words and their being
          how they come into their signifying.

St John's is seated somewhere on the southeastern coast;
          what sense of direction does direction afford?

          What of life's soft nudge and bump?

          These are not questions for a confession.

12.4

Christ Church felt like a homecoming after the years of absence.
So was St Paul's Church—there, you walked straight into sanctity.

"I have heard thousands of confessions, but never one of covetousness."

That's what St Francis Xavier said about what people have to say.

          How could that have been, you think to yourself,
          how could no one have coveted?

How can anyone today look beyond what we desire,
          that excess and greed?

5.18

So was St Paul's Church, I confessed.

On a hill so slight, you look up and think you're walking home.

I like to tell people the body of St Francis Xavier was temporarily buried
here in 1553.

He'd died in Shangchuan Island, China.

I went to Malacca to see the open grave of my patron saint
          before he became my patron saint.

His body was eventually shipped to Goa,
which also felt a bit like home.

24.13

Which year was it when I received the relic of St Francis Xavier? It was sometime between 2006 and 2008. My bedroom had rosaries decorating its walls, hung from small nails. They were made of beads of every kind—glass, plastic, crystal, pearl, moonstone, olive wood, sterling silver, steel, seed. They draped across the wall, beaded curtain. Last year, I received two more rosaries, one limestone and the other Job's tears from wild adlay.

I wanted to give some rosaries away, but they remain too precious. Before I die, I will donate the relic to church, along with every other precious Catholic thing now in my keep.

The Litany of St Ignatius of Loyola called him—

encouragement to all our scholastics
model of interior peace
living always in God's presence
within a long list of attributes

What do names and relics do for the saint, and for the adherent?

0.31

Have you enjoyed your swim today?

I can't remember, Daddy says.
I can't remember, the second declaration like desperation, its gasp.

Daddy drops his head back into the deep of the pillow.

On good days, he remembers to recite the psalms.

Mother's skin looks like pastry, flaking, red spots where she breaks skin, as if to draw blood from a life of pride and fierce individual freedom. The givenness of autonomy.

Yet, no one gets to choose the consequence of free will.

Who are the men and women of goodwill;
more importantly, who discerns—

> who are the men and women of good faith?

24.14

What do words and objects do,
when they serve their most rarefied function?

> The Litany of St Francis Xavier called him—

> > prophet mighty in word and works
> > wonderful worker of miracles
> > preacher of the truth and doctor of the nations
> > amidst a long list of enumerated names

Look at the bronze medal. The front depicts St Ignatius of Loyola, and the reverse St Francis Xavier. The medal was made in a Roman foundry in the 1700s. It was made for the Society of Jesus. The metal, strike, and image are all correct for that period.

JHS or IHS is a Christogram, Latin in short for Jesus Hominum Salvator, or Jesus Savior of Mankind. This is a distinctive Christogram. The reversed S—2—is another version of the letter within the Latin alphabet. 2 substitutes for S, it's said, to reflect a child's longhand, that first attempt at a different kind of signifying practice.

That initial shift between textualities,
            from text as speech to text as writing.

9.1

Perhaps you can tell more
            about someone (and anyone)
            from how one has lived one's life
                        than what one actually says.

> Nothing is an availed destiny—
> what might someone think of this?

Then again, there is the spiritual certitude.

(I try to pray novenas right through the year,
          an endless suite of Spenserian stanzas,
          always closing with the alexandrine line.)

There is spiritual discipline with spiritual certitude.

          And always a humbling of the spirit,
          there's that too.

How daily devotions at once bear and arrive, how they come into view.

                            Nothing is known,
until one comes into the eventual, certain knowing.

Of destination, good or pained—
          endless and enduring,
          either way.

But, there's still the prayer for the dead,
          the souls of our dear and faithful departed.

There's still that, and what we make of confession and reconciliation.

     And always,

          the Blessed Sacrament tomorrow,
          you already know.

        ....

        ....

        ....

Amidst Compline and Prime

"If a man wishes to be sure of the road he treads on,
he must close his eyes and walk in the dark."

Saint John of the Cross

as much as this lyric seems so faraway
inasmuch as distance is nearness

as much as that night seems as removed
inasmuch as tomorrow's dawn is arrival

as much as this utterance feels out of reach
inasmuch as love demands an idiom

as much as that sufferance feels impassable
inasmuch as hope rests on our faith

DAILY
EXAMEN

PROSPECT

Holy Silence, Praise Song

Anywhere, up to each point in time and meaning
when sense took flight—airborne, heaven-bound.
God always, between and within nowhere/thereto
pauses. Only ever holy love, now here, now-here.

A Reference Point

"Come to Me, all who are weary and heavy-laden, and I will give you rest."

Matthew 11:28

I kiss the top of my Holy Bible, lips against leather, along edge.

I am writing again, and the squall has settled.

Into restful night.

Oh, the silence. The breathless, the stormless.

The pastoral is writing itself out, like an open field.

Did it state atonement,
as if already steadied and preparatory?

(Yes, I said *atonement*, the second life of penance.)

Yes to the humbling—

to such work
raised
to The Work,
how conscious,
how conscientious
the working
out of what matters.

Yes, yes to what sanctifies.

A promise repeated so many times
—in admonition, at times, to make stark.

Like stature, of holy relic.

A reminder suggested, to self and story.

THE DAILY EXAMEN

Set aside good time for your Daily Examen.
Be aware that you are in the presence of the Holy.

"Trust in the Lord with all your heart,
and do not lean on your own understanding.
In all your ways acknowledge Him,
and He will make your paths straight."

Proverbs 3:5–6

Write.

"May the God of hope fill you with all joy and peace
as you trust in him, so that you may overflow
with hope by the power of the Holy Spirit."

Romans 15:13

Poem Epilog:
Hereinafter, Lines of Longing

"God always wins. If you are his instrument,
you too will win, because you will fight God's battles."

Saint Josemaría Escrivá, *The Forge*

I.

Every poem henceforth
must be bright light—

> this reflective sound,
> like I said.

> Like I say today.

II.

This and that, the way of language.

III.

And resolutely,
the contemplation of the years
> —the long years—
> and how they come
> and go.

IV.

Within my heart,
in the depth and ground of things,
> always
> the steadfast faith.

> God in front of me,
> and foregrounded.

V.

As it was written and so goes always,
Exodus 14:14—

*"The Lord will fight for you,
and you have only to be still."*

VI.

What will this moment become,
and what of the next, and its next,

as awake in the light?

That shimmer
—of Truth—
its eternal echo.

VII.

Each line within,
each poem carved into form,

as emphatic.

To iterate
language as hearthstone
and home of being—

abiding love
of form,
of Truth—

like I said.

As I say.

VIII.

As if it was there all along,
and how the light lets itself in—

like morning
always.

APPENDIX:
Examen Drafting Log

Catachresis, Then Catechesis	[First Version on Fri, 18 Nov 2022, 11:01pm]
The Difference of Sounds	[First Version on Fri, 18 Nov 2022, 9:08pm]
Poem Prolog: Hereinafter, Along the Line	[First Version on Mon, 19 Oct 2020, 4:37am]
The Daily Examen	[First Version on Tue, 11 Jun 2024, 4:35pm]
The Year Ash Wednesday Fell on Valentine's	[Final Version on Tue, 26 Dec 2023, 6:21pm]
Tintinnabulation	[First Version on Sun, 25 Oct 2020, 1:02pm]
Dear Impressionism	[First Version on Fri, 15 Jan 2021, 11:45pm]
Tintinnabulation II	[First Version on Sun, 25 Oct 2020, 1:34pm]
Leavings for Poor Sojourners	[First Version on Wed, 11 Jan 2023, 3:56pm]
Rose Window, Baptistère Saint-Jean	[First Version on Thu, 26 Jan 2023, 2:05pm]
Blind Country of the Dying	---
Ecclesiastes 4:4	[First Version on Tue, 6 Dec 2022, 8:13am]
Recompense for the Novelty of Gossip	[First Version on Tue, 13 Sep 2022, 3:44am]
	[Second Version on Fri, 28 Oct 2022, 5:46pm]
Field Notes on the Flaming Heart	[Revision on Fri, 14 Jun 2024, 10:15am]
Dear Blue-Eyed Cat	---
Scene of Saint Martin: Monostich Catalog	---
Necessity 101	---
Dear Saint Matilda—The Slight Evidence	[Revision on Fri, 14 Jun 2024, 10:27am]
The Contingency of Saying	[Revision on Fri, 5 Jul 2024, 9:14pm]
Eternal Motion	[Revision on Fri, 14 Jun 2024, 11:01am]
Conversation on Mount Olivet	[First Version on Wed, 17 May 2023, 4:44pm]
[Absent Extant Poem]	---
Saint Josemaría Escrivá's Donkey Theology	[Revision on Tue, 11 Jun 2024, 12:22am]
Jerusalem Donkey Waiting for the Cross	[First Version on Tue, 13 Sep 2022, 3:43am]
	[Later Version on Tue, 11 Jun 2024, 9:32am]
Mangy Donkey Sestina: A Triptych	[First Version on Fri, 28 Oct 2022, 1:43pm]
[Absent Extant Poem]	---
Vista // Vision // Visitation	[First Version on Thu, 18 May 2023, 11:30pm]
What I Saw at the Sepulchre of St Mary	[First Version on Mon, 10 Jul 2023, 7:45am]
	[Second Version on Mon, 31 Jul 2023, 12:43pm]
	[Third Version on Tue, 11 Jun 2024, 12:36am]
The One Happy Thing	[First Version on Wed, 23 Nov 2022, 8:47pm]
The Tallest Speech Act of All	[First Version on Fri, 6 Nov 2020, 2:37pm]
Knowingness, Signs, Professions	[First Version on Mon, 19 Oct 2020, 4:58am]
	[Later Version on Tue, 18 Apr 2023, 12:07pm]
Lazarus the Friend of Christ: Larnaca	[First Version on Wed, 28 Dec 2022, 1:18am]
Christ's Tear for Lazarus: Abbey of la Trinité	[First Version on Tue, 27 Dec 2022, 7:36pm]
The Cross of Hope: Church of Agios Lazaros	[First Version on Wed, 28 Dec 2022, 3:31pm]
Reading Poetry in St Lazarus Church, Yangon	[First Version on Fri, 6 Jan 2023, 4:46pm]
Fr Gabriel's Oboe	[First Version on Fri, 6 Nov 2020, 3:00pm]
	[Later Version on Mon, 21 Jun 2021, 3:30pm]
Small Acts of Translation	[First Version on Fri, 6 Nov 2020, 8:04pm]
Translation Memory, Principle of Reduction?	[First Version on Fri, 6 Nov 2020, 8:20pm]
After Chiaroscuro	[First Version on Sat, 7 Nov 2020, 2:22pm]
Tenebrism Again, In Relief	[First Version on Sat, 7 Nov 2020, 7:07pm]
The Act of Movement	[First Version on Sun, 8 Nov 2020, 2:43pm]
Fides Quaerens Intellectum	[First Version on Fri, 27 Nov 2020, 1:07pm]
Triptych: Iteration of Only Importance	[First Version on Wed, 2 Dec 2020, 2:20am]

Dignum Memoria

At the point of publication, I wondered whether this drafting log should be included.

I unearthed some text that I penned for the Issue 73 INTERVENTION feature of *Voice & Verse Poetry Magazine*. Published on social media as background to my poems, these insights help shed light on how this need for documentation came to be.

What memories does my mind latch onto, which ones decide to find voice in lyric actuality? What kinds of memories seem more pressing, or less pressing; and yet, demand a kind of articulation? Am I conscious of the nature of these memories, and indeed, how my mind understands its own relationship with memory? The work of memory—the function of its meanings, the values we accord, our ability to sit with our own memory, and so many other remarkable things. These are the questions that fascinate me now, in my work as a poet.

My habit of dating my poems, as well as significant revisions, only began a few years ago. It's an effort to understand my own writing process, how memory locates itself in time and language and context, and how a poem may evolve its own constructions. Recently, I stumbled on some article about how memory may adjust itself, change, even correct itself over time, as a way to help us survive our own past. I like the idea of it. That our own memory can hold space for us.

My poems surprise me upon rereading. That, too, is an effect I like. I recently reread one of my poetry collections from ten years ago, and was astonished at how differently I found myself reading my own work. I recall the contingency I afforded my lyric during the writing of individual poems, as well as the selection and compilation of them for the book proper. Yet, so much meaning came through as new, beyond the matter of origins, in the most luminous, gratifying ways.

Often, I'm simply glad and grateful I put word to thought and emotion— had I not got up, to sit at my desk to type these lines out, the poem would never have been made. In fact, just this early morning, I was moved, by the Holy Spirit, to force myself out of bed, to write down all that was going on in my mind. What emerged were three poems, driven through a string of couplets, with concluding lines variously loosed, almost in controlled release. It was the most absorbing hour, an hour well-spent.

I enjoy this return to a poetry of inspiration, where the compulsion to create comes from beyond the self. The urgency becomes almost a demand, better yet, a duty. That I'm more confident in how to shape my lyric language— even if the newness of this voice constantly surprises me—really helps, by way of the ease with the writing. I feel less tethered to technical virtuosity or a poem's performativity. I feel freer as an artist. I feel a closeness between who I am, and my poetic creation. I feel a greater ownership over the materiality of my lyric.

Consequently, it's made me a happier poet. My poems are not a challenge or battle I set up for myself, something to surmount. My poems are an extension of the self—expression, as idiom of the self, a finer diction that seems glad and gratefully content to have found itself on the page.

That is the intervention. The intervention of poetry in the fragile sense of who we are in our own lives. In this vast world, and what gentle poetry we make of it.

NOTES

✸ In 1522, Saint Ignatius of Loyola conceived the Daily Examen as he was writing his Spiritual Exercises. The Daily Examen is a much loved technique, inviting one to commit dedicated time to prayerfully reflect on the events of the day. This brief examination of conscience helps us feel God's presence in our lives, to seek out God's grace, to develop spiritual discipline, to discern God's direction for ourselves, and to offer thanksgiving and praise for our many blessings.

✸ "The Year Ash Wednesday Fell on Saint Valentine's Day" first appeared in *Poems for Ephesians*. In 2024, Ash Wednesday coincided with Saint Valentine's Day. This poem is inspired by Ephesians 2:4–5: "But because of his great love for us, God, who is rich in mercy, made us alive with Christ even when we were dead in transgressions—it is by grace you have been saved."

✸ "The Difference of Sounds" was read at the Singapore Writers Festival in 2022, for the panel "What If We Break the Rules?".

✸ "Leavings for Poor Sojourners" was read for the Australian podcast, *Death and Donuts*, in an interview with Sebastian James.

✸ "Dear Impressionism" was produced as a video poem in 2021 for World Anthropocene Manifesto, organized by École Urbaine de Lyon, Université de Lyon.

✸ "Field Notes on the Flaming Heart" was penned as a response poem to Glory Ann Balista's "Flaming Heart", with both poems published in the anthology, *Call and Response*.

✸ "Eternal Motion" was written specially for the event, *In Stitches*, and performed at the National Gallery Singapore on 28 January 2018.

✸ Jaffa Gate remains one of several ancient gates of the Old City of Jerusalem. It also goes by the names of David's Gate, Hebron Gate, and Gate of the Friend. Tradition has it that the prophet Jonah set off on his sea journey from the port of Jaffa.

✴ "Jerusalem Donkey Waiting for the Shadow of the Cross" works off the intriguing trait of donkeys having a cross right across and down their back, really spectacular when viewed from a high angle. The piece is a poetic reauthoring of a small Christian fable of the Jerusalem donkey, and the origin story of the cross on its back. In the Holy Bible, the donkey is one of very few animals with a speaking line. My poems look at the donkey as a symbol of humility and service.

✴ "Mangy Donkey Sestina: A Triptych Dismantled & Reconstituted" is a fun word experiment that takes all the difficulty out of writing the formidable sestina, while being attentive to its structural requirements. The epigraph of Zechariah 9:9 notes the prophetic fulfillment of Jesus' entry into Jerusalem seated on a donkey.

✴ These donkey poems are inspired by the Spanish priest Saint Josemaría Escrivá, who founded Opus Dei. In 2002, he was canonized by Pope John Paul II. I was really moved by his life and thought after reading Mariano Fazio's *Last of the Romantics: St. Josemaría in the Twenty-First Century*. Saint Josemaría's own book, *The Way*, has sold millions of copies internationally. The saint is known for his dictum, which he lived by: "Pure mathematics: Josemaría = mangy donkey."

✴ Apart from *The Way*, Saint Josemaría's *The Forge* and *Furrow* have offered beautiful research for various poems, alongside other spiritual readings like Saint Francis de Sales' *An Introduction To The Devout Life*, Saint Teresa of Avila's *The Interior Castle*, and Saint Thérèse of Lisieux's *Story of a Soul*. Epigraphs and quotations have featured excerpts.

✴ Deep gratitude goes to the many thinkers whose lives or words have left their impression on me over the years. Several are mentioned here, their thought appearing as axioms or epigrams on occasion. These include: Bishop Robert Barron, Caravaggio, Dejan Stojanovic, Father Andrew Dalton, Father Mark-Mary, Father Mike Schmitz, Fanny J. Crosby, Frank Bidart, G. K. Chesterton, Gerard Manley Hopkins, Hans Urs von Balthasar, Helen Keller, John Bacchus Dykes, Jonathan Roumie, Judith Beveridge, Karl Barth, Lorine Niedecker, Ovid, Peter Kreeft, Pope Benedict XVI, Pope Francis, Reginald Heber, Robert Creeley, Saint Anselm of Canterbury, Saint Augustine of Hippo, Saint Catherine of Siena, Saint Frances Xavier Cabrini, Saint Francis of Assisi, Saint Francis Xavier, Saint Gertrude of Nivelles, Saint Ignatius of Loyola, Saint John of the Cross, Saint Martin de Porres, Saint Matilda of Ringelheim, Saint Monica, Saint Patrick, Saint Pio of Pietrelcina,

Saint Peregrine Laziosi, Saint Rita of Cascia, Saint Rose of Lima, Saint Thomas Aquinas, Salvador Dalí, Simone Weil, Walter Benjamin, Virgil.

✳ The poem, "Vista // Vision // Visitation", relates the two apparitions I saw in 2016 at the Church of Saint Anne and earlier, at the Tomb of the Prophets. Deep gratitude to the National Arts Council and Nanyang Technological University for kindly affording me their writing residency, which allowed me precious time to write, and to take this research trip to Jerusalem.

✳ "What I Saw at the Church of the Sepulchre of Saint Mary: Scene XVIII" appears here as the sole installment within an audio transcription of, at last count, some seventy-seven confessional speech acts. This involves a recount of a Marian apparition I witnessed at the Tomb of the Virgin Mary.

✳ "The Tallest Speech Act of All" and "Translation Memory, and Your Principle of Reduction?" were read for the Poetry on the Move Festival 2021 feature, "Working the Archives". Poetry on the Move is organized by the Centre for Creative and Cultural Research at the University of Canberra.

✳ The account of Jesus miraculously raising Lazarus from death, four days after his entombment, also appears only in the Gospel of John. Lazarus resided in Bethany with his sisters, Martha and Mary. Several traditions mention Saint Lazarus becoming the first bishop of Marseilles in France, as well as the bishop of Kition or Larnaca, in Cyprus.

✳ "A Reference Point", "Blind Country of the Dying", "Postmeridian Dalí II", "Tenebrism Again, In Relief", "The Act of Movement", and "Tintinnabulation II" were performed at the opening reading of Poetry on the Move Festival 2022, for which I was invited as an International Featured Poet.

✳ "Fides Quaerens Intellectum", "Postmeridian Dalí", and "Triptych: Iteration of Only Importance" were read and recorded for Poetry Festival Singapore, in a special Advent reading series. The twelve-feature reading marathon spanned the first Sunday of Catholic200SG and Christmas Day. This final twelfth installment was published on the third day of the Nativity Triduum. The other featured authors included Gerard Smyth, Marjorie Evasco, Angela Alaimo O'Donnell, G. C. Waldrep, Joshua Ip, Jenni Ho-Huan, Julie Moore, and Eric F. Tinsay

Valles. All the writers across the twelve installments were published in *A Given Grace: An Anthology of Christian Poems*, which was exclusively created to commemorate the Philippine Quincentennial and Singapore Bicentennial of Catholicism in 2021. Featuring 100 writers from across the world, *A Given Grace* was showcased at the Catholic200SG Festival Luminary Art Exhibition.

✳ "The Cross of Hope: View From Church of Agios Lazaros" refers to St Lazarus' Church, one of the earliest churches in Macau, China. It was constructed between 1557 and 1560. The Cross of Hope is preserved in the current building, as a remnant from the original chapel.

✳ "Tenebrism Again, In Relief" was inspired by Ephesians 1:18–23: "I pray that the eyes of your heart may be enlightened in order that you may know the hope to which he has called you, the riches of his glorious inheritance in his holy people, and his incomparably great power for us who believe. That power is the same as the mighty strength he exerted when he raised Christ from the dead and seated him at his right hand in the heavenly realms, far above all rule and authority, power and dominion, and every name that is invoked, not only in the present age but also in the one to come. And God placed all things under his feet and appointed him to be head over everything for the church, which is his body, the fullness of him who fills everything in every way."

✳ The epigraph to "Ordinary Time" features the opening lines from Pope Francis' homily for the Solemnity of the Epiphany of the Lord in January 2023.

✳ The elements within "Sonnet to Adoration of the Holy Eucharist: List Poem" are elaborated on in the document, "The History of Eucharistic Adoration: Development of Doctrine in the Catholic Church" by John A. Hardon, SJ.

✳ "Amidst Compline and Prime" was inspired by Ephesians 2:13: "But now in Christ Jesus you who once were far away have been brought near by the blood of Christ."

✳ It is a rare and precious occasion when Singapore is graced with a visit from the Vicar of Christ. In 1986, Pope Saint John Paul II made a trip to the city-state, an island country. With its timely publication, the first edition of *Heart Fiat* is dedicated to Pope Francis, to mark his visit to Singapore in September 2024.

PREVIOUS PUBLICATIONS

Deep gratitude to the following publications where these poems, some in their earlier versions, have previously appeared:

A Given Grace: "After Chiaroscuro"
"Fides Quaerens Intellectum"
"Postmeridian Dalí"
"Tintinnabulation"
"Triptych: Iteration of Only Importance"

As Surely As The Sun: "A Reference Point"
"The Difference of Sounds"

Atelier of Healing: "A Reference Point"
"Fr Gabriel's Oboe"

Ballast Journal: "Scene of Saint Martin:
Monostich Catalog"
"Vista // Vision // Visitation"

Borderless: "The Contingency of Saying"
"Eternal Motion"

Call and Response: "Field Notes on the Flaming Heart"

Ekstasis: "Ordinary Time"

eratio: "Overheard at Walled Churchyard"

Fare Forward: "Lazarus the Friend of Christ:
Larnaca Tomb Inscription"

Foreshadow: "The One Happy Thing"

Notre Dame Review: "Catachresis, Then Catechesis"

Nur Melange: "Rose Window, Baptistère Saint-Jean"

Of Zoos: "Vista // Vision // Visitation"

Poems for Ephesians: "The Year Ash Wednesday Fell
  on Saint Valentine's Day"
"Amidst Compline and Prime"
"Tenebrism Again, In Relief"

Porch Literary Magazine: "Reading Poetry in St Lazarus Church,
  Yangon"

Quarterly Literary "Conversation on Mount Olivet"
Review Singapore: "How Did Fish Become This Hour,
  This Narrative Memory?"
"Lazarus the Friend of Christ:
  Larnaca Tomb Inscription"

Rabbit: "Small Acts of Translation"

The Jesuit: "Episodic Memory,
  What Memorabilia-Made-Explicit"

To Let The Light In: "Blind Country of the Dying"

Valiant Scribe: "Translation Memory,
  and Your Principle of Reduction?"

Voice & Verse: "Holy Silence, Praise Song"
"Jerusalem Donkey Waiting
  for the Shadow of the Cross"
"Mangy Donkey Sestina: A Triptych
  Dismantled & Reconstituted"
"Tintinnabulation II"

ACKNOWLEDGMENTS

My heartfelt thanks to:

The Arts House, Ministry of Education, National Arts Council, National Gallery Singapore, National Library Board, Poetry Festival Singapore, Singapore Book Council, and Sing Lit Station for providing me such invaluable opportunities over the years. Thank you for having me onboard to conduct various literary events, where I was able to share the importance of art, literature, reading, writing, among many good things. From such readings and workshops were birthed ideas and texts that have attained their polish for publication here.

This lovely press for believing in my work, and bringing this book to life. Thank you for your openness, kindness, respect, professionalism, and just being so awesome to work with.

The eminent authors who penned cover praise for this book. You have totally made my day, and I adore your work.

The lovely artists whose beautiful works grace this collection. Your art is nothing short of stunning.

In my previous books, I listed more than two hundred individuals by name, and expressed gratitude for how they had helped me in some manner throughout my work as an artist.

For fear of unwittingly leaving out anyone, I would like to thank everyone who has been an important presence in my life, and helped me along this strange and wonderful journey.

This includes all my teachers at Harvard University, University of Notre Dame, and National University of Singapore. Your guidance was invaluable.

My colleagues at Nanyang Technological University. Thank you for being so good to work with, for creating such a collegial, warm, open space for all of us to do our scholarship.

Our literary scene tucked up here in Singapore. Gratitude to everyone whom I've met at all these fabulous literary events. Thank you for the splendid conversations, your encouragement and/or previous insight into my work.

My students, many of whom have become fond friends, for the beautiful discourse and keeping me on my toes.

My lifelong friends, you know who you are. For the years! Thank you for accepting me, even at my most reclusive, ridiculous, and impossible.

My dear parents, siblings and larger family. Thank you for always being there, and for keeping me grounded and humble.

Especial mention goes to Eric Francis Tinsay Valles, whom I'm chuffed to bits to call my godfather. Your prayers, Eric, are the most precious gifts you could ever give me. I trust you completely.

The priests at Novena, Risen Christ, Saint Joseph's Victoria Street, and Saints Peter and Paul. Of The Work, Fathers Joe Lopez, Derrick, Frank, Michael, Joseph D., Avelino. Thank you for your boundless patience and important counsel. You help me in my walk toward a life of holiness.

F. X., short for Saint Francis Xavier. As with all my previous books dedicated to you, this book is written for you too, my dearest patron saint. I will always happily bear your name as my baptismal name.

Non nobis Domine non nobis,
Sed Nomini tuo da gloriam
Sed nomini tuo da gloriam.

Mother Mary, my unceasing thanks for your mighty intercessions. Thank you so much for always being a Mother to me.

Above all, God, for all His provisions. My eternal gratitude, Lord Jesus, for guiding me steadily throughout this creative process. Thank you for always blessing me so abundantly, beyond my wildest imagination. None of this beautiful life would have been possible without Your Grace.

Without You, God, I am nothing, and can do nothing.

You alone are my rock and my salvation.

AUTHOR

DESMOND Francis Xavier KON Zhicheng-Mingdé (b. 1971) is the author of an epistolary novel, a quasi-memoir, two lyric essay monographs, four hybrid works, ten poetry collections and a guided creative journal. A former journalist, he has edited more than twenty books and co-produced three audio books, several pro bono for non-profit organizations.

Trained in publishing at Stanford University, Desmond studied sociology and mass communication at the National University of Singapore, and later received his theology masters from Harvard University and creative writing masters from the University of Notre Dame.

In addition to grants from the National Arts Council and Singapore International Foundation, Desmond has enjoyed literary appointments at the Notre Dame Poetry Fellowship, NAC Gardens by the Bay Writing Residency, and NTU-NAC Creative Writing Residency. Among other accolades, Desmond is the recipient of the IBPA Benjamin Franklin Award, Singapore Literature Prize, Poetry World Cup, two Independent Publisher Book Awards, two Illumination Christian Book Awards, and five Living Now Book Awards.

Desmond has taught writing for over two decades, his contributions recognized with the Hiew Siew Nam Distinguished Academic Award and four teaching excellence awards. For the most part, Desmond tries to preserve an unhurried, quiet, hermitic life.

desmondkon.com